Arsenal 'Til I Die

Arsenal 'Til I Die

THE VOICES OF ARSENAL SUPPORTERS

Edited by David Lane

Meyer & Meyer Sport

British Library Cataloguing in Publication Data
A catalogue record for this book is available from the British Library

Arsenal 'Til I Die
Maidenhead: Meyer & Meyer Sport (UK) Ltd., 2014
ISBN 978-1-78255-038-9

© 2014 by Meyer & Meyer Sport (UK) Ltd.
Aachen, Auckland, Beirut, Budapest, Cairo, Cape Town,
Dubai, Hägendorf, Indianapolis, Singapore, Sydney, Tehran, Wien
Member of the World Sport Publishers' Association (WSPA) www.w-s-p-a.org
Printed by: B.O.S.S Druck und Medien GmbH, Germany
ISBN 978-1-78255-038-9
E-Mail: info@m-m-sports.com
www.m-m-sports.com

CONTENTS

INTRODUCTION

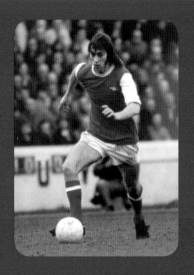

I am very happy to be writing the introduction to this book. Arsenal is my boyhood club, and I was lucky enough to go on to play for the team I support. I grew up at Highbury on the North Bank terraces, watching players such as David Herd, Joe Baker, George Eastham and John Radford, so I know just how important the club is to the fans, and, as a player, I played for those cheering me on.

The level of support for Arsenal never fails to amaze me. I was born in Islington, so I know how strong our local support is. Now, as a tour guide at Emirates Stadium, I meet fans from all over the world who have just as much passion for the club. When I meet supporters from overseas who have travelled over here for a match, and I think about how much money they must have spent, it always amazes me. Getting to watch the match live means a lot to them. I'm no different; it is well known that I once pretended to be ill when selected for the reserves, so I could travel to watch the first team in an FA Cup tie away at Bristol City. And I've had friends who have missed weddings and hospital appointments to go to matches without giving it a second thought! The Arsenal is a special club, and it is so because it is superbly well run, from top to bottom, and I am proud to still be a part of it. I hope you enjoy reading this fantastic book. Up the Gunners!

Charlie George

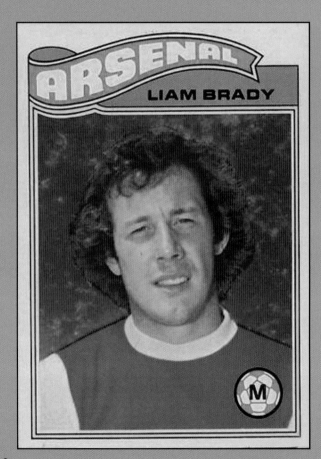

ARSENAL

LIAM BRADY

WE CAN DO IT!

Growing up as an Arsenal fan in the late 1970s and early 1980s was a frustrating yet (occasionally) exhilarating experience. One of my earliest memories is of watching the 1979 FA Cup Final when we beat Manchester United 3-2, thanks to a dramatic last-minute winner from the Afro-haired Alan Sunderland. This after we had led 2-0 for most of the game, only to let United get back to 2-2 and seemingly gain the upper hand as extra time beckoned. I can still remember John Motson's commentary as Liam Brady tried one last surge forward: 'There's a minute left on the clock, Brady for Arsenal... right across... Sunderland! It's there! It's 3-2!' A wonderful memory.

I was, perhaps, a bit too young to fully appreciate the thrill of an FA Cup win. I was not quite seven years old, so I didn't realise at the time that it was Arsenal's first major trophy win in eight years—since the Double-winning team of 1970/71. Nor did I realise it would be our last major trophy for eight years—until George Graham's young Gunners won the Littlewoods Cup against Liverpool in 1987.

As I became more emotionally involved in Arsenal's fortunes and attached increased importance to the club's results, the highs and lows became increasingly stark. I could never rationalise those feelings (I don't think any die-hard football fan could), and even now, more than 30 years later, I am still no closer to understanding how the game of football can make the heart race or the stomach knot to such an extent. I recall a desperately painful 4-3 League Cup fourth round defeat at Third Division Swindon Town in 1979, when it seemed like we were certain to win. In fact, 1979/80, the first full season I remember properly, was one of the longest and most tiring in the club's history—a season that promised so much but ultimately delivered sweet nothing!

Three replays were needed to beat Liverpool in the FA Cup semi-final, so surely a final against Second Division West Ham wouldn't pose too many problems. But 10 May 1980 was the first day of the rest of my Arsenal-supporting life. Memories are now snapshots: a blazing hot day; an underperforming Brady, Stapleton and Rix; a stumbling, scrappy, headed goal from Brooking and a cynical foul on 17-year-old Paul Allen by Arsenal's hard-nosed Scottish stopper, Willie Young, which almost certainly denied the then youngest ever FA Cup finalist a special goal. We lost 1-0, and I was inconsolable.

That defeat was bad enough, but surely salvation would come the following Wednesday when Arsenal faced Valencia in the European Cup Winners' Cup final held at the Heysel Stadium, Brussels. Again, I have snapshot recollections of that evening: a tense, cagey affair, not much goalmouth action, my mum stunning us all by shouting an expletive as Alan Sunderland had a goal disallowed for offside in extra-time (probably the last time I ever heard her swear) and, finally, my first exposure to penalty shootout heartbreak.

Pat Jennings kept out the first penalty, taken by Valencia's Argentine World Cup winner, Mario Kempes. Liam Brady, my favourite player, stepped up to take our first spot-kick. Surely he wouldn't miss. But Chippy couldn't convert. Carlos Perreira, the Valencia keeper, guessed the right way (and moved way before the kick was struck), so Arsenal's advantage was immediately cancelled out. Eventually, we reached sudden death, and a nervous-looking Graham Rix had to score to keep the shootout going. Perreira guessed correctly again, and, despite my dad's cries that he moved early again, the Cup was on its way to Spain. Two finals, two defeats.

As Arsenal approached their 69th and final game of a seemingly never-ending season, we knew that a win at Middlesbrough could possibly clinch the last UEFA Cup place from Ipswich Town. By this time, however, the players were running on empty. Midfielder Brian Talbot was apparently on the brink of collapse after the 5-0 hammering at Ayresome Park. We had to settle for fourth place. There would be no European football for Arsenal the following season.

I was learning that there was a very fine line indeed between agony and ecstasy when it came to supporting Arsenal, and there was worse to come. I was aware of rumours that Liam Brady was getting restless, and there had been talk of a move abroad. As an eight-year-old who idolised the man, I think I was in denial. I refused to believe that he would leave. He couldn't leave, could he?

It was while we were on our annual family holiday to Scarborough, in July 1980, that I heard the news I had dreaded: Liam Brady was to sign for Italian giants Juventus for £600,000. How much? Hadn't Trevor Francis been signed by Nottingham Forest for over £1m? How on earth could Brady be allowed to leave for a little over half that amount? To me, the valuation was a case of insult being added to injury.

The season 1980/81 was a quieter one for Arsenal. It lacked the drama and excitement of the cup runs. Spurs and Everton saw to it that we were eliminated from the League Cup and FA Cup early. New boy Kenny Sansom even scored an own goal in the defeat at Goodison Park.

However, it was a noteworthy season for me because Boxing Day 1980 saw my first ever trip to an Arsenal game when my dad took me up to Selhurst Park to see our encounter with Crystal Palace. I remember being excited to see Pat Jennings in the flesh but disappointed that Stapleton was unfit and couldn't play. The game finished 2-2, with Willie Young having a spectacular over-head kick goal disallowed in the last minute—for dangerous play! My most vivid recollection, however, was of the serious trouble that broke out on the Holmesdale terrace at halftime. Scores of people seemed to be falling down the steps of the terrace, thanks to the violent frenzy. We were safely seated way over in the Arthur Waite stand, but my dad struggled to reassure me that they wouldn't be coming to get us! Little did I know that these scenes were commonplace at that time in English football.

A third-place finish in the league meant a place in the UEFA Cup the following season, but the departure of Stapleton that summer, for £900,000 to Manchester United, was another sign that the club was struggling to compete with the 'big boys' and couldn't match the ambition of some of the bigger name players. What followed was a period in the doldrums; defeats at the hands of Walsall, Winterslag and York City were notable lowlights in the coming years. Not until the arrival of George Graham in the hot-seat in 1986 did things begin to change.

The Gunners found glory again under Graham and, of course, later under Arsène Wenger, but it is those formative years that instilled that love, that unconditional devotion to the cause. Somehow, even in the direst of circumstances, as a true Gooner you always have at least a faint hope that a seemingly lost cause can be remedied. Logic is often absent in the mind of the die-hard supporter. 'We can still do it'; 'If we beat them, then draw with them, we could still do it.' From the age of 7 to 37, a part of me always believed Arsenal could do it, and this will never change.

Stephen Rusbridge

GOOD OLD ARSENAL, WE'RE PROUD TO SAY THAT NAME

Friday, 26 May 1989, a day not only never to be forgotten in Gooner history, but also a preface to the modern Arsenal. Here is my story of the evening and why I think it changed the face of our fabulous club. The run-up to the game is embedded in the history books, but no one can effectively describe the disbelief and despair that echoed around Highbury following the 2-2 home draw to Wimbledon. We had a 12-point lead over Liverpool at Christmas and had seen it whittled away to being three points behind. We had thrown away five home points in two games against poor oppositpproachedion. We had choked. Goodness knows the furore had there been blogs in those days—Samaritans would have been busy!

The drudge home after the Dons game was very long. I gave little hope for our chances at Anfield and didn't even try to get a ticket, but, as the game approached, I dug deep, sought some 'mental strength', found some fighting spirit.

It should be noted that the 'crunch' game on Mersyside was on a Friday night—unheard of in those days and rare now. My wife, thinking that football was a Saturday sport, had booked us to go to a dinner party at her new boss's (let's call him Rupert) flat in the centre of Hampstead. She worked in the media business, and all the guests were from Saatchi & Saatchi. I told her that I couldn't attend unless I could watch the game through dinner. Her response was to tell me to call Rupert. And here we come to the huge social change that came about that night, and in my opinion changed the face of football forever.

This was the season of Hillsborough; the reputation of English football fans was at an all-time low. If you liked football, you were considered violent, ignorant and uncultured. Football was for yobs. Rupert, being cultured and polite, was delighted to hear from me and said that as a guest, of course, I could watch the game, but... I would have to sit at the table with the sound off and participate in the conversation.

We arrived and were shown into a beautiful dining room with a long table, and I was sat at the end with a separate table for my 14" TV. I felt humiliated and less-than; however, my addiction came first, and I was satisfied. The host had caterers to do the food and serve the wine, allowing him to concentrate on his guests. Needless to say, I was at the opposite end of the table to him, due to his assumption that my passion must mean I was incapable of enriching any intelligent conversation. Seriously, to those young people who read this, football fans were viewed as stupid. There were no university courses in Sports Management, no Soccer Academies.

So, the first half comes and goes, and I am getting tense. At halftime people were very 'nice' to me, commiserating as though I had lost a pet. Champagne was flowing around the table, some guests snuck off to the toilet and I sat there non-communicative, wishing I could find somewhere dark to be alone. The second half kicked off. Smudger scores. I jump up shouting; they look at me as though I have escaped from a psychiatric unit, BUT—and here is the start of the change—they got caught up in my passion. Rupert asked me to turn the TV so he could see it. Questions were asked: 'Who is the tall bloke who keeps raising his arm?'; 'Why don't they shoot more?'; 'Why, when Arsenal play in red and white, are they playing in yellow and blue?' Needless to say, I was incapable of speech.

The Mickey T moment never ever to be forgotten. It replays in my mind in slow motion (as I am sure it does for you). The whole table went mental, jumping in the air, hugging, back-slapping and shouting. My main recollection was thinking: 'Where is my coat, I have to get to Highbury...' But Rupert and his friends were high on the game. They had really enjoyed watching a half of football. They connected! If Big Raddy—a less thuggish man you could never meet—was a football fanatic, it couldn't be just razorblade-toting thugs that went to Highbury. I am ashamed to say that I 'liberated' a couple of bottles of bubbly, grabbed the wife and skedaddled as fast as I could to N5. I was dropped off outside the Gunners pub, carrying the champagne, which lasted about four minutes. *Fever Pitch* got it right: There was an enormous street party, a feeling of camaraderie never repeated. The noise was deafening, and I stood on the marble steps until around 3am. Even at that time, the Holloway Road was awash with jubilant Gooners, sharing laughter and booze. Fantastic.

I met Rupert and a number of the fellow guests over the following seasons. All had bought season tickets at Highbury and were as knowledgeable and connected to the Arsenal as any Gooner. Football had become the drug of the masses!

This is what *The Guardian* wrote of the game and the social effect it had: 'Many cite the match as a pivotal turning point in English football.' Writing in *The Guardian*, Jason Cowley notes how instead of rioting, as had occurred at Heysel with fatal consequences, Liverpool fans stayed on after the game and applauded Arsenal 'as if they understood that we were at the start of something new; that there would be no returning to the ways of old'. Cowley describes the match as 'the night football was reborn' and that the event 'repaired the reputation of football'.

The match is not only seen as the starting point of a renaissance in English football, but also the moment where people started to see the untapped commercial potential of live football on television. 'Good old Arsenal, we are proud to say that name.'

Big Raddy

IN THE LONG RUN

When I was a child, I was fascinated by the European Cup and was desperate for the day when Arsenal would be in it. Back in the 70s, before the expanded Champions League, I knew that day may take quite some time to arrive. So, I made a pact with my young self that if that day ever arrived, a time when we were in the world's premier tournament, then I would go to every game, home and away, until we won it. What was I thinking? I had no idea what I was getting myself into.

It all started so innocently in Lens. We had a great team in 1998, a fantastic manager and we were playing all our home games at Wembley. I was certain that Arsenal were going to blaze their way through the tournament, and I would be there to see Tony Adams lift the trophy, which would be job well done! But maybe I should have seen the signs when Lens equalised in injury-time. Things got worse, though, as it became apparent that Arsenal weren't as good as I thought they were, and the Gunners were unceremoniously dumped out by Fiorentina in the group stages.

This was my first experience of a now annual condition which is known as 'Champions League Depression', which starts with the grim realisation that Arsenal are about to get knocked out, again. The symptoms often worsen and turn into anger at the players and manager; then the depression really kicks in because of the pact I made and the realisation that I will have to go through it all over again. I start to ask myself: 'Will I ever be free of this curse?' The depth of my depression also gets worse year by year as I get more and more anxious to be free at last.

The early years were the best as I visited many new cities and countries and met many new friends along the way. It was all new and exciting, and I sensed that our team was simply too good not to win the trophy—but every time we were let down. And every year my obsession worsened and my desire for the team to win grew greater. One year, my girlfriend at the time actually asked me to miss a game to go on holiday with her—the cheek of it! She gave me a straight choice between the holiday and her or the run. Shall we just say my run is still going! There have obviously been lows and highs along the way, emotions which I am sure we have all shared, but, then, just as I was losing faith and starting to consider the unthinkable and throwing the towel in, the Champions League run of 2005/06 came along to tease me, and

the sight of Jens Lehmann diving to his left to palm away Riquelme's penalty in Villarreal actually brought me to tears. Finally, I was going to see Arsenal in the Champions League final, and I was 90 minutes away from glory—the day that my personal run would finally be completed.

Paris was the best and worst of days all rolled into one. The excitement during the build-up was wonderfully emotional for me, but, oh, the disappointment that followed was almost unbearable. But a funny thing happened to me when I looked up to the stadium clock on 75 minutes, when we were 1-0 up. I suddenly thought to myself: 'Arsenal are 15 minutes from winning—my run will be over, and this is as good as it is going to get!' I have to admit that I panicked and actually felt sad—a weird, mad feeling! I then realised that the run had taken over me, but hey, not to worry, because a couple of minutes later those masochistic thoughts quickly disappeared. We all know what happened next, eh? And so, as I write this in June 2010, my run now stands at 127 consecutive Champions League games not out, and I am truly desperate for it to come to an end. Yes, I really am! Maybe I was not ready in Paris, but I am now on bended knees, begging Arsenal to put me out of this misery. I have lost girlfriends and missed work and travel opportunities in becoming a complete slave to the run, yet the end still seems further away than ever.

Because of the run, I have been forced into becoming a relative part-timer for domestic away-game duties when compared to amazing fans like Andrew Miller, John Williamson, Chris Cannon, Mario and Colin The Cap, but I ask of you, if the glorious Champions League winning day ever arrives for the Gunners, please spare a thought for me and my fellow victims. I think there are just under 10 of us who are on similar 'unbeaten' runs, so, smile, raise your glasses in the knowledge that I have finally been set free.

Adam Velasco

THE DAY I TOOK GEORGE EASTHAM TO LUNCH

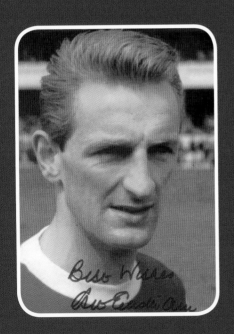

Best Wishes
Best Eastham

George Eastham (No. 41 of the Arsenal greats, born George Edward Eastham on 23 September 1936 and made an OBE for services to football) was the outstanding midfielder of his day and served as Arsenal captain between 1963 and 1966. One of the things that stands out in my mind to this day is that he was such a visionary that it took his Arsenal team-mates about 18 months to learn how to play with him. He would frequently pass into an open space only to find that his team-mate had failed to cotton on; he was capable of the finest of defence-splitting passes. He was a great sportsman and hardly ever committed a foul. He was the Liam Brady or Cesc Fàbregas of his day—though probably not so prolific a scorer.

Eastham also played for England and made the 1966 World Cup squad, but not Alf Ramsey's team, as well as playing for Newcastle United before and for Stoke City after he played for Arsenal. He remains to this day one of my favourite players of all time.

Those of you over the age of 50 may, like me, remember George with some fondness, too, but not only was I fortunate enough to see him play for the Gunners, I also was lucky enough to take him out to lunch.

In 1959, towards the end of his contract with Newcastle United, Eastham had made it clear he was unhappy with Newcastle and refused to resign a contract. He wanted to go to Arsenal and asked for a transfer. The Geordies refused to let him go, though, and relied on the rule at that time that permitted a club to block any move because they owned the player's registration, and they did not have to pay him either, because he had requested a transfer. It was in fact nothing less than old-fashioned slavery in modern times.

Although Newcastle eventually relented and sold him to Arsenal in October 1960 for £47,500, George rightly believed that there was a principle at stake. Backed by the PFA, who stumped up his legal fees, he briefed the leading barrister of the day, Lord Gardiner, who later became Lord Chancellor. The point was whether it was right that any employer could prevent a person from plying his trade or—to put it in legal terminology—was the retain-and-transfer system a 'restraint of trade'?

So we had the top footballer and the leading barrister and what would undoubtedly be a leading case on freedom of contract. Now it just so happened, at that time, that I was

SUN SOCCERCARD No 249

G. EASTHAM (England)

not only a passionate Arsenal supporter, whose hero was George Eastham, but also a keen law student, who loved the law of contract and aspired to be a barrister. So, to kill three birds with one stone, so to speak, I thought I would go along to gaze on my hero, George, close-up, listen to the top advocate of the day and maybe even witness legal history being made.

In the courtroom at the High Court, the attendance figure was particularly low and, apart from the lawyers and the judge, the only people in court were George and me! At lunchtime, I waited to see if George would be surrounded by hangers on, lawyers or other parasites. But no! He was ignored and looked slightly lonely. I approached him and invited him to have lunch with me. We went over the road to the nearest pub, appropriately called The Seven Stars, where I spent a really pleasurable time with him. I am pleased to say he was both intelligent and charming as well as being a perfect gentleman.

My last and abiding memory of George Eastham is when Billy Wright dropped him to the reserves so was forced to watch his magic being regally conferred with the stiffs.

Incidentally, George won his case. The High Court ruled that the retain-and-transfer system was an unreasonable 'restraint of trade' and thus illegal, and the case remains important among lawyers to this day!

Laurence Kingsley *pictured on page 21 with his father in 1971*

THE FOOTBALL ASSOCIATION CHALLENGE CUP COMPETITION

FINAL TIE
Arsenal v Liverpool
SATURDAY, APRIL 29th, 1950 at 3 pm

OFFICIAL PROGRAMME · ONE SHILLING

The Empire Stadium
WEMBLEY
Chairman and Managing Director:
SIR ARTHUR J. ELVIN, MBE

MY FIRST CUP FINAL

I was born in 1938, so I was seven when the Second World War ended. My earliest recollections of going to a football match were in 1946 when I was taken to White Hart Lane, which were in fact an Arsenal 'home' fixture, as the club had been forced to share Tottenham's ground for a season due to bomb damage to Highbury. Thankfully, the following season, Arsenal were back where they belonged, and I was taken on a regular basis thereafter.

However, despite having earlier memories of watching Arsenal, it's 29 April 1950 that has been indelibly imprinted in my brain for over 60 years—the date of my first Arsenal Cup Final. Imagine my emotions when I came home from school on Friday evening and my father tells me that he had managed to obtain two tickets for the following day's FA Cup Final: Arsenal versus Liverpool. I don't think I slept that night with the excitement of it all.

We headed off to Wembley early the next morning and were among the first to enter the stadium when the gates were opened, my father wanting me to experience every aspect of the occasion, starting with the massed bands marching up and down the pitch. This was followed by the community singing, led by Arthur Caiger, culminating in the emotional singing of the traditional Cup Final anthem, 'Abide With Me'. The fact that it had been raining steadily all day and that I was soaked through in no way detracted from my enjoyment, although I'm not sure my father felt the same way. However, all this was forgotten with the arrival of the teams and the kick-off.

I can remember Liverpool looking dangerous early on, mainly through their talismanic figure, Billy Liddell, who was known as the Flying Scotsman. However, our right-half, Alex Forbes twice let Liddell 'know he was there' as they now euphemistically say, and the winger was never the same threat again that day. The pendulum had swung, and we had a perfect view as Jimmy Logie threaded a wonderful pass through for Reg Lewis to slip the ball past the advancing keeper for Arsenal's first. I can still see that goal as clearly in my mind as I did on the day. Lewis scored again in the second half, and we were never in danger after that. Arsenal had won the Cup! I think I slept even less than the previous night, as I relived the whole day in my head.

Since then I have enjoyed many Arsenal triumphs, not to mention numerous disappointments, but nothing has ever eclipsed the memory of my first Cup Final and, to that end, I would like to thank my late father, coupled with the names of George Swindin, Laurie Scott, Walley Barnes, Alex Forbes, Leslie Compton, Joe Mercer, Freddie Cox, Jimmy Logie, Peter Goring, Reg Lewis and Denis Compton.

Peter Clydesdale

AND SO IT GOES ON

I have been an Arsenal supporter since 1963. My dad's 10th birthday present to me was a trip to Highbury to see Arsenal play Sheffield Wednesday in the FA Cup; we won 2-0, and I was hooked. However, my story relates to events that took place some 10 years later. In fact, the date was 24 February 1973—an away game against Carlisle United, which Arsenal won 2-1. My late father, my elder brother and I were chased back to the station by Carlisle fans after the game where we had to catch the football special back to London, but disaster struck as we hared our way along the platform. My brother stepped on the heel of my shoe, which came off and fell on the track under the train!

Instinctively, and with no obvious regard to my safety, my dad and my brother grabbed hold of my legs and dangled me under the train in an attempt to retrieve my shoe. As I fished about and stretched my arm towards the stray piece of footwear, the train let out a big 'SHHHHHH' noise, meaning that everyone panicked, but, as they quickly pulled me up, I not only emerged alive but I had the shoe in my hand! Dad gave me a massive hug, but we had a train to catch, so we set off at a brisk pace and boarded the train as quickly as we could.

Because we were the last to board, the train was so full we could not find a seat, despite walking from the front to the back, then all the way back again, meaning there was no option other than to sit on the floor all the way back to London. Despite the lack of creature comforts, we sat and sang the praises of our glorious Gunners. I remember most of the chat revolved around Carlisle's Ray Train, who had taken out Peter Storey, and, as Storey was carried off on his stretcher, you could clearly make out the injured Gunner telling Sammy Nelson 'Get him!'

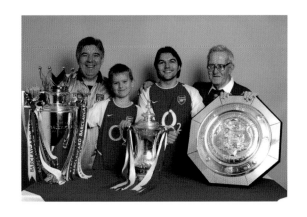

[Left] The Robinson family

Arriving back at King's Cross was somewhat of an anti-climax—the end of a big, highly-anticipated Arsenal day out was always like that—and as the Gunners fans dispersed in every direction, we made our way to the Underground to get the District Line towards Dagenham Heathway. We hid our scarves at Upton Park just in case West Ham fans got on—as many of you will recall you had to take precautions like that back in the 70s.

Being a teenage Arsenal fan 40 years ago was one massive adventure with all those different cities to explore and discover, even though we were often treated like cattle. The three of us went to every home and away game throughout the 70s, and my mum would send us off with a packed lunch, which was more like a hamper in reality, and my dad had a ritual of saying, 'Who's got the tickets?' as we got on the train. He would then whip out two tickets and say he had left mine (I was the youngest) behind. We would always laugh as if it was the first time he had said it!

My dad was a character and is missed by us all, but I have had a stone laid at Armory Square in his memory, and my own son and his boys now come with me to the Emirates. And so it goes on, as hopefully it always will.

Terry Robinson

SUPPORTING WHERE HIPPOS RUN WILD

I hail from Karungu Division of Migori district, Nyanza province, Kenya, which is one of the remotest places on Earth, and an area without electricity or piped water. My comrade Arsenal fans and I usually trek over 12km to be able to catch a glimpse of our favourite team—braving torrential rains, night-runners, cops, wild animals and thugs just to watch our heroes. The Champions League matches are usually screened here at around 21:45 – 22:45 East African time, depending on the season. Picture three people trekking through jungles and wildernesses to have been able to watch the likes of Keown, Campbell or Vermaelen. Arsenal is our passion: We live it every second of the day, every day of the year.

One Champions League day, my friends Fanuel Otieno Opon, Nicholas Chida Obondo and I set off to watch Arsenal take on PSV Eindhoven. It was raining cats and dogs on our way to our destination, and we had armed ourselves with clubs and machetes in case we met the hyenas or the foxes. Eventually, we met the hyenas, but luckily they were busy with their taste buds and teeth tearing a dead animal apart. Eventually we reached our venue, dripping like gutters and were forced to watch the match wearing only our boxer shorts as we had stripped to allow our clothes to dry. After the game, we went to check our clothes, but they were nowhere to be seen. The time was 01:15, but we had no choice other than to set off home regardless. Unfortunately, on our return journey we met the police patrol who arrested us for being in possession of dangerous weapons and having no identification documents, and because we were out walking at odd hours of the morning, I was forced to buy our freedom by parting with my hard-earned weekly wages, which in English money amounts to around £10. We battled on through the night, but the paths we were following were extremely heavy with mud, and deep-water puddles were everywhere. At one point, we had to swim across a 150-metre-long field full of water, which had pooled from the surrounding hills. The next bridge was impassable, as the water had burst its banks and the current was too strong to attempt, so we had to backtrack towards the lake hoping to find a shallow point, which we never found. This meant that the only option we had was to swim the crocodile-infested lake. We eventually reached home at 05:30 where, cold and exhausted, I had to spend the next two days bedridden because of fatigue.

So, next time you walk into Emirates Stadium, imagine me wearing my Nasri top where jackals, foxes, alligators, crocs and hippos run wild and are the order of every night. Arsenal is my team; I live for their flair, passion and spirit—it's Arsenal 'til my grave.

Odero Duncan Otieno [*pictured left*]

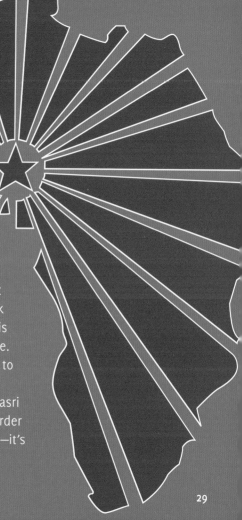

THE ITALIAN JOB

It was 23 April 1980, two weeks after the Highbury draw against Juventus, and, with the score supposedly against us, I was one of only 500 or so travelling Gooners brave and probably mad enough to fly out to Italy for the return match. And, not only did we walk the same streets in which the classic *The Italian Job* was filmed but, more importantly, I savoured what is one of the most amazing nights of my life.

I'm sure all those aboard the early morning flight out to Turin were full of very mixed feelings and emotions. I felt excited about heading off to the home of one of the greatest teams in the world and had every intention of making the most of the day, come what may. After all, this was the Cup Winners' Cup semi-final second leg!

In truth, after the 1-1 home draw, with Juve's away goal to take into account, and the fact that no English team had ever won in Italy and that Juventus had never lost a home European tie, it meant my expectations were more of hope rather than expectation. I wasn't banking on Arsenal reaching the final at the end of the night's play. However, the hours leading up to the game were brilliant.

The Juventus fans seemed friendly enough, and the Turino fans were even friendlier and made it clear they wanted Arsenal to win. By a great stroke of luck, we stumbled upon a bar owned by a Turin fan, and, magically, all the beers were all free! When we arrived at the ground, we were greeted by a full house where 80,000 fanatical Italians were screaming—not at the match, but at 500 Gooners that had been herded together like sheep in one small pocket of the stadium.

The game itself was a non-event for 75 minutes, with Juventus more than happy to play out a goalless draw, which was all they needed. But then the excitement started. With just 15 minutes left on the clock, a young, inexperienced 18-year-old kid by the name of Paul Vaessen came on for Arsenal and, with the clock ticking down, a left-wing cross from Graham Rix was met by the substitute, who headed past Italian goalkeeping legend Dino Zoff. The Gooners went barmy, but the remaining 79,500 fell silent (although we were certainly treated to plenty of stares) until the final whistle went, when it felt like an impossible dream had came true!

Judging by the reaction of the locals, a 1-0 Arsenal win was certainly not in the script, and, as the jubilant Arsenal players left the pitch, the next difficult task was for the 500 to get out of the ground in one piece, which at that time could not be taken for granted. We were all held back until Carabinieri reinforcements arrived to help get us out safely. With a double line of riot police holding plastic, reinforced riot shields above our heads to form an improvised 'roof', we all moved as one beneath our human shield as bricks

and bottles came raining down. In fact, the Arsenal fans present that night owe a debt of gratitude to the police as, without their help, I'm sure I may not be here to relive this tale.

Once aboard the coach, it was time for a full police escort back to the airport with sirens screeching, lights flashing and red traffic lights jumped all the way—it was clear that the coach drivers had been told not to stop for anything, or anyone!

Thankfully, there was no hanging around at the airport, and, as soon as we arrived, our plane was ready to rock 'n roll with priority clearance. Within seconds of boarding our aircraft, the doors had been shut, and we were up in the air where we all breathed a huge sigh of relief and the most amazing celebrations erupted at 30,000 feet. It was party time all the way home, because, to my surprise, we were on the same plane as the Arsenal players, the management team and many board members—now that's what you call the icing on the cake!

I still look back at that night as one of the greatest in the club's history, and I'm sure that the Gooners that were lucky enough to be there, along with the thousands listening on the radio back home, would all agree. That win will live with me for the rest of my life.

Gary the Gooner *pictured with his son, Gary the Gooner Jr.*

A NORTH LONDON ODYSSEY

Like many football fans, the football club I have been a lifelong supporter of was not made by elective choice. It was something I inherited by birth. I grew up on a housing estate in Islington. Highbury stadium, the 'Home of Football', was a brisk 15-minute walk across Highbury Fields. My father was a lifelong Arsenal fan. Hence, I inherited a passion for football directly from him and spent my childhood dreaming of becoming a centre-forward for Arsenal Football Club.

On the estate where I grew up, ball-games were forbidden, but this did not prevent us 6- to 10-year-olds playing one-touch games in the tight confines of the yard. We also had access to the 'Cage', a dedicated area of tarmac surrounded by high wire mesh fencing. As a kid, I would devote hours to playing footy with my mates in such venues. Being left-footed, I styled myself on my hero, Liam Brady. But the fact that we were left-footed was about all I had in common with Liam, and my footballing prowess never progressed beyond that of Sunday morning pub-team level.

The earliest relocations of my interactions with Arsenal are dimmed by age, sparse and scant. I remember being taken to a game by my dad at Highbury in the 1969/70 season. We sat in the lower East Stand. The opposition were Wolves; we drew 2-2, and Derek Dougan scored both goals for Wolves. Among other early memories is watching from my dad's shoulders on the corner of a packed Clock End as Charlie George headed a winner against Leicester City just before halftime in an FA Cup replay in 1971.

I also remember listening to second-half commentary on BBC Radio Two as that late penalty from Peter Storey at Hillsborough secured a 2-2 draw and replay against Stoke in the semi-final of that same season.

But most clearly of all, I remember watching the 1971 FA Cup Final on TV as an eight-year-old, and, when Charlie drove in that extra-time winner, I jumped onto my nan's lap and hugged her with delight. In the years following the Double season, I became a regular at Highbury, rarely missing a game until I left North London and went to university.

But as a nine-year-old, my friends and I started watching from the schoolboys' enclosure. Often, one of our parents would walk with us across Highbury Fields and leave us at the kids' entrance while they went onto the North Bank. As I was quite short, I only saw intermittent patches of the play and relied on my older and taller mates to give me piggybacks during parts of the match so that I could see. As I got a little older, about 12 or so, we were allowed to go over to the match alone. Invariably, though, I'd be at Highbury a good three hours before kick-off so that I could secure a spot at the front of the schoolboy section, which was directly in front of the East Stand in those days, adjacent to the North Bank. Between us and the pitch was a concrete wall and a deep moat. Still relatively short for my age, I was only able to see with difficulty beyond the wall and spent most of the games in a rather uncomfortable position of lying with my stomach on top of the thin slither of wall.

My team idols in those days were all forwards: Radford, Kennedy, Graham and George Armstrong, and, in those days, football-crazy kids like myself would play football all day before school, during playtime breaks and after school, too. We would collect and swap the season's football stickers, gluing them into albums. The BBC's 'Match of the Day' on Saturday night and ITV's 'Big Match' on Sunday afternoons were essential viewing and provided us with an opportunity to see highlights of our teams; then, at school on the Monday, we'd argue endlessly about whose team was best and try to emulate the moves we'd seen. One season, as kids of my generation will remember well, everyone was trying to do an 'Ernie Hunt'. In the latter seasons of Bertie Mee's reign as manager, I started to watch games from the Clock End, which also provided access to the west side standing area. Often, we'd walk down along the west side and find a spot close to the North Bank. The west side had a short metal fence separating us from the pitch and provided a far better view.

In the mid-70s, football hooliganism was starting to emerge as a serious problem, and I have distinct memories of watching us beat Manchester United 3-1 and West Ham 6-1 with huge numbers of opposition supporters occupying large swathes of the Clock End terraces. These were dark days indeed, when Arsenal occupied the lowly reaches of the First Division in the 1974/75 and 1975/76 seasons; although, I remember that Brian Kidd had been signed, and he enjoyed a good swan song to his career, scoring many goals for us in those seasons. I particularly liked a skilful forward called Alex Cropley, who had a frustratingly injury-hit career. However, Armstrong and Radford remained stalwarts at the club, and at one evening match, Radford hit a late winner that was long celebrated on the North Bank. I remember staying behind on the west side and watching as the North Bank sang jubilantly for some 20 minutes after the game had ended. Although the incident is not highlighted in the Arsenal history books, that goal against the would-be champions Liverpool reinforced our belief that relegation in the 1975/76 season would be a virtual impossibility.

At the age of 14, in Terry Neill's first season as manager in 1976/77, I at last felt old enough to stand on the North Bank. It was great as my friends and I stood in the central sections of the terrace either in the thin section at the back or the mid-section itself. This area became packed with young teenagers such as us, and we chanted and sang all game long. 'We hate Nottingham Forest', 'You are my Arsenal', 'Knees up Mother Brown', 'Maybe it's because I'm a Londoner', and a corrupted version of the West Ham 'Bubbles' anthem were the flavours of the day. There was always great delight and pandemonium of jumping bodies as we celebrated any Arsenal goal as 'Super Mac' ably led our line and the young Irish trio of Brady, O'Leary and Stapleton were establishing themselves as the spine of the first great Arsenal team that I have distinct memories of. My spell on the North Bank was brief, though, as it soon became much 'cooler' to be associated with the Clock End. Perched predominantly on the east side of the clock, we were close enough to trade direct and immediate banter with supporters of the visiting team, and it was as a 15-year-old that I started to go to my first away games.

For longer distance journeys to places such as Old Trafford, the City Ground or Hillsborough (for the first leg of one memorable FA Cup third-round tie), we would jump aboard the travel club's special trains, and we'd all be met by large cordons of police officers who would frog-march us to the grounds. For London games at Spurs, West Ham and Chelsea, everyone would gather at one pre-arranged station, then travel like sardines packed on Tube trains and arrive en masse. For games against Midlands teams such as Coventry and Villa, or 'shire' teams such as Ipswich and Southampton, we'd get an 'away-day' ticket and travel in such numbers that we'd easily out-sing the home fans. Terry Neill's teams were always very competitive, and the 'SAS' forward line of Stapleton [pictured right] and Sunderland was ably supplied with opportunities from the sublime skills of Brady and Rix. Price, Gatting and Talbot provided graft to the midfield, while O'Leary and Young formed a formidable central pairing with Rice and Nelson, providing width and solidity either side of them.

An evergreen Pat Jennings proved agile and reliable in goal. Neill's Arsenal always finished in the upper half of the table, and I have some treasured memories of that era, particularly the games at White Hart Lane. I was there on the Park Lane when Brady drove in that stupendous strike in the 5-0 thrashing in the 1978/79 season. I was at the Paxton a season later when, with a team boasting 'six reserves', we beat them 2-1 with late goals from Paul Vaessen and Alan Sunderland. However, that team is best remembered for its Cup exploits that resulted in three successive FA Cup Finals between 1978 and 1980, plus the Cup Winners' Cup Final, and I was there for all of them, including the semis beforehand—what great seasons!

In my eyes, the highlight of the 1978 run was the semi-final at Stamford Bridge when Rix scored our third in front of a packed Shed End. At Villa Park the following season, we watched from the right-hand side of the Holt End as a second-half brace from our SAS pair saw us past Wolves, and the semi-final of the 1980 season saw us travel regularly up the M1 motorway—Hillsborough, Villa Park (twice) and then, ultimately, to Highfield Road where we celebrated Talbot's header early in the first half. On the morning of the Cup Winners' Cup Final, I, like many other Gooners, awoke slightly the worse for wear in an Ostend B&B, but the town's flat sandy beaches hosted impromptu kickabouts for the hordes of expectant Gooners killing time before their coach departures to the Heysel stadium in Brussels later that afternoon. Obviously, the proudest memory of all from this spell is of standing on the high steps of the Wembley terracing when

Alan Sunderland rescued us from stunned disbelief with his last-minute goal to send us cavorting into a wild melee of delight.

I spent the 1981/82 to 83/84 seasons in self-imposed exile from North London while I was at university, but during the breaks between terms, I would always return home and visit Highbury. Admittedly, these weren't vintage seasons for the Gunners, but I can recall sitting in the upper East Stand for a game against Villa when Vladimir Petrovic drove home a stunning 20-yard winner, and, also vividly remember standing on the Clock End and applauding Spartak Moscow from the field after they'd cut us to ribbons with a hitherto unseen style of fast-flowing football. I also witnessed Walsall beat us 2-1 in the League Cup, which I'll happily skip over, except to say that it was a defeat that was to precipitate the departure of Terry Neill.

Charlie Nicholas arrived at the same time that I returned back from uni, and my friends and I, now in our early 20s, would gather on the west wing of the North Bank to watch an infuriatingly inconsistent team. We'd spend many an hour in the pubs in North London, analysing and discussing a post-mortem of the games. In Arsenal's centenary season, George Graham's first as manager, I at last had wheels of my own, and a group of us would travel to almost every away game as George's young charges set the season alight. A 22-match unbeaten run saw us at the top of the table for several months, and I remember our game at Old Trafford, when Norman Whiteside led the assault, literally, on the Arsenal team.

Unpunished challenges led to the game boiling over, which culminated in an enraged Rocky getting sent off, and, at the end of the game, Viv Anderson needed to be visibly restrained as the opposing benches vented their spleens in what was to become an increasing volatile fixture. That 2-0 defeat and the disappointing run of form that followed it confirmed George's cautious public declarations that the team would not take the title in his first season. It was to be the Littlewoods Cup that would provide glory. We had tickets in the seats at the Park Lane end for both the semi-finals at White Hart Lane, where the atmosphere was electric and the noise phenomenal. The intensity of the emotional rollercoaster of those fantastic ties was energy-sapping, and it is almost impossible to describe the intensity to those that weren't actually there. We were also at Wembley where 'El Pel's' sublime touch and burst of pace to set up

Charlie's second in the final against Liverpool took place directly in front of the seat I occupied that day. Then, in the 1987/88 season, a couple of my friends and I set up the Arsenal fanzine *One-Nil-Down, Two-One-Up* that was a popular read at Highbury for over a decade of seasons, and I regularly submitted articles to the early editions and helped sell the magazines outside the ground before the matches.

Like many Arsenal fans of my generation, I'd been just a little too young to fully appreciate the 1970/71 title-winning season, hence the 1988/89 campaign was particularly magnificent and at last proved to be the one that finally realised my dreams of seeing the Gunners lift the League Champions trophy. I found the intensity of my own focus on that Anfield match almost unbearable in the days preceding the game. The nerves got to me so much that I decided not to travel to the game, and I even refused to watch the match with the friends that I had travelled all over the country with following Arsenal for years. Believe it or not, I watched ITV's broadcast of that famous night on the TV at home with my dad and my brother Steve, but Mickey's late strike was absolute perfection. Completely overjoyed and beside ourselves, we hurried over to the Alwyne Castle where we joined the lads and sang on the streets outside until the small hours of the morning.

For the remainder of George's tenure, I regularly watched the games from the comfort of the East Stand Upper, and the memories of those trophy-laden seasons could fill a book in themselves. However, as I entered my early 30s, my attendance at matches started to gradually decline. My eldest two sons were born in 1994 and 1995, respectively, and, over the three years between 1994 and 1996, I was studying in the evenings, working long days in my full-time job and adapting to the challenges of fatherhood. Something had to give. My love for the club never waned, even though I was forced to follow most of the games via Capital Gold where Jonathan Pearce's excitable commentary allowed me to 'multi-task' the ironing (or such-like) and keep up to date with the Arsenal score. Then, when Sky arrived and took over football coverage, I would visit friends or go to the pub to watch matches involving Arsenal, which is how I looked on and celebrated when Arsenal secured Arsène Wenger's first title with that 4-0 demolition of Everton at Highbury. The FA Cup final of that same season was the first one involving Arsenal that I had not attended live since we lost 1-0 to Leeds in 1972. Instead, I watched the game on TV at the bedside of my father who was enduring the last few months of a terminal illness, and, despite the sad circumstances, strikes from Overmars and Anelka cheered us both.

My attendance at live Arsenal matches was precluded even further for the 1998/99 to 2003/04 seasons as I spent just over five years living and working abroad, although the availability of satellite television allowed me to keep in touch with the progression of Wenger's Gunners. In fact, I was probably able to see upwards of 75% of all the Premier League games that Arsenal played in the seasons spanning my time abroad! We returned to the UK in the summer of 2004, and, after settling into our new home in Hitchin, I was able to continue my 'armchair' vigil via Sky TV coverage of Arsenal's progress under Wenger. A smallish stadium capacity, long waiting list for season tickets and a packed membership scheme were all barriers to getting to see a live match at Highbury. Times had changed significantly since I could simply stroll over the park and pay cash at the turnstiles. However, being once again so close, a strong desire to return to the Arsenal fold started to grow.

On Boxing Day 2004, my family were at my mum's for some traditional festive fare, and Arsenal were due to play Fulham at home. Despite the fact I didn't have a ticket, I could resist temptation no longer and decided to stroll over to Highbury, following a well-trodden route across Highbury Fields, to pick up a programme from one of the sellers outside the Clock End turnstiles. It was a nostalgic stroll, and, on my return journey, I bumped into several friends I hadn't seen for ages. We exchanged Christmas salutations as they made their way to the game—but it had got me thinking.

Some work colleagues allowed me the use of their season ticket when they were otherwise engaged, and, in the 2004/05 season, I was able to visit Highbury twice, where I saw both a Thierry Henry inspired 4-1 victory over Norwich and a Dennis Bergkamp inspired 7-0 victory over Everton from the West Stand Upper. The 7-0 win will go down in history as the last Highbury appearance of Patrick Vieira in an Arsenal shirt, which he capped with a delightful finish for our third goal. It was ironic, as most of the focus that night

was on an emotional farewell to Edu (who we knew was bound for Valencia) and a 'fear' that we might be witnessing Dennis' final bow at Highbury.

That evening, Bergkamp gave a performance of such mastery that it became virtually unthinkable he would be released. I was grateful for my colleagues' generosity, too, in the 2005/06 final season at Highbury, as from the same perch in the West Stand Upper I was able to witness the Premier League games against Man City, Liverpool and West Brom, as well as the Champions League semi-final first leg against Villarreal. The 1-0 victory over Man City witnessed the Pires-Henry penalty shambles that will become one of those 'What happened next?' questions on future TV shows. Against Liverpool, a brace from Thierry Henry secured a 2-1 win: the first a brilliantly bent shot around Reina following a sublime through-pass from Fàbregas and the second a neat finish following a gifted back-pass by Steven Gerrard.

The game against West Bromwich Albion had been assigned the theme of 'fans' day' by the club. The 'fans' chose to forgo that honour, instead dedicating the game to Dennis Bergkamp. A plethora of fans wore specially commissioned orange T-shirts for the day. Dennis Bergkamp came off the bench with 15 minutes to play and the score at 1-1.

He coolly kept his head in the 6-yard box to set up Pires for our second goal and then curled in a trademark drive of his own from the edge of the box for our third. Along with the squirrel, the game against Villarreal was my live debut at Highbury for a Champions League match. The atmosphere was electric, and, although a lot of the game was quite tactical, the Highbury crowd held their nerve, recognising that a clean sheet was as important (if not more important) than scoring a second goal. However, I guess the proudest moment for me personally that season was the League Cup tie against Reading. When the tickets went on general sale, I was quick off the mark to purchase four seats in the East Stand Upper. It gave me the opportunity to take my three sons to their first live Arsenal game and allow them their only visit to Highbury, too. We were rewarded with a 3-0 victory as van Persie, Reyes and Lupoli supplied the goals.

After a certain amount of procrastination and deliberation early in 2006, I enquired about and eventually

purchased two season tickets at Club Level for the inaugural 2006/07 season at Emirates, and I am proud to say that I have retained them ever since, and I have enjoyed watching as Arsène's young team have gone in search of that elusive first trophy in our new home. In truth, the seats stretch our budget to its limit, but it has given me an opportunity to share my passion with my four children as I 'rotate' them through games so that all can share in trips to Emirates.

Following Arsenal has given me so many moments of pleasure, and whether it is following them live up and down the country as I did until my early 30s, or following them predominantly from the comfort of an armchair, as I did until we moved to Emirates, I still get that buzz of anticipation in the build-up to matches. I still cannot rest during a match, wherever I may be, until I have learned the final score, and I still enjoy spending hours analysing the strengths and weaknesses of our current squad and am happy to share my insight and history of the club with anyone who has the patience to listen! There are many uncertainties in life, but one thing is for sure: My passion for Arsenal will remain with me until my dying day.

Brad Duncan

GETTING SHIRTY WITH ARSENAL

Sibling rivalry was always a big thing in my family, and, as the youngest, I was determined to get the better of my brother and sister as often as I could. Even an innocent game of Snakes and Ladders could turn into a fiercely contested battle for us. As such, it should come as no great surprise to hear that each of us supports a different football team.

Back then, we lived near the Kings Road, and so, by rights, I should be a Chelsea fan. But my sister, being the eldest, had beaten me to it. She was cheering for Chopper Harris while I was still in short trousers, while my brother had chosen to support Bobby Moore's West Ham. Hardly a surprise given that this was the late 60s.

When my turn came to start following football, I looked around for a team that I could call my own. Both Fulham and QPR were close by, but, regardless of their proximity, I chose Arsenal—mostly, it has to be said, because it was a station on the Piccadilly Line. Sad, but true! Of course, that decision turned out to be a stroke of genius in the first year or so, as the Gunners went on to clinch the Double. But then it happened! When my parents bought me my first replica kit in 1971, little did they know what it would ultimately lead to later in life!

Back in those days, the Arsenal cannon was on a separate patch, which had to be sewn onto the shirt, and, although Umbro included an iron-on number in the box, you couldn't choose which one it was. My shirt came with the number 7, and I'll admit I was a little disappointed that it corresponded with Geordie Armstrong rather than Charlie George. George was definitely my favourite, and the fact that my parents

hated his long hair just made me like him even more. Still, the number thing was no big deal really. I loved that shirt, and I wore it with pride for several years until it finally fell apart.

I continued buying the replica shirts whenever they became available, although I did miss out on a few during my poor student days. So a few years ago, I decided that it was time to fill in the gaps in my collection. I just wanted 'one of everything'. How hard could that be? And so I took my first step onto the slippery slope of serious shirt collecting.

I guess you need to understand that I am a very detail-oriented person (with some rather trainspotter-like tendencies); therefore, my definition of 'everything' kept on expanding. After buying the shirts I was missing, I decided that I also wanted all of the long-sleeved shirts to go with the short-sleeved ones. Plus, there were the goalkeeper shirts, obviously. Then I wanted the players' shirts as well as the replica versions (yes, they're different). After that, there were the Premier League shirts, the Champions League shirts, and the right- and left-handed versions of the shirts. OK, I made that last one up, but hopefully you get the picture. If you look hard enough, you'll find that there are a huge number of different Arsenal shirts out there. And don't even get me started on the special ones used in the Cup Finals.

I have to hold my hand up and say that, at some point, my hobby became more of an obsession, and I now spend hours every week poring over the newest eBay listings, searching in vain for some of the more elusive shirts. I'm not alone either! I've got to know a number of other shirt collectors over the years, and I'm pretty certain they all bid against me when something particularly juicy becomes available. My wife thinks I'm a nut, of course, and I think that she may have a point. I mean, who needs 250 Arsenal shirts that they never wear? These things cost money, they take up a lot of space and there's that familiar and strangely unique 'football shirt aroma' about them too. Old football shirts seem to acquire a distinct smell over time, which no amount of Persil ever gets rid of.

Don't get me wrong, my shirt collection is not grounds for divorce (well, not yet anyway), but it doesn't exactly promote marital harmony either. Let's just say that there have been a few awkward moments, like the time my wife discovered just how much I had paid for a rare shirt. She almost cancelled our holiday, and I was conscious to be on my best behaviour for quite some time afterwards.

And on several occasions my wife has asked me what, eventually, I am going to do with all of my shirts. It's a fair question, but one that I really struggle to answer. You see, much as I love my Arsenal shirts, they are essentially useless. And I can't take them with me when I die, either. My head says that she's right and that I should probably just sell them at some point, but my heart isn't quite ready to lose them all quite yet—not for a while anyway. No, I won't rest until my collection is finally 'complete', even though I realise that may never happen. Besides, next season is Arsenal's 125th anniversary, and it's highly likely that there will be some splendid new commemorate shirts to mark the occasion, so for now I'm still chasing my bizarre dream of owning every Arsenal shirt from 1970 to the present day. And if any of you know the whereabouts of an 82/83 or an 86/87 long-sleeved away shirt, then please let me know...

Peter Rapley

Fellow Arsenal shirt anoraks can view Peter's amazing collection here:
http://picasaweb.google.com/ArsenalShirts

NOT IF,
BUT WHEN...

'Never a penalty... never! I can't even watch... Oh God, Oh God... Lehmann, I'll never say a bad word against you again if you pull this off, you nutter... YEEEESSSSS! WE'RE GOING TO PARIS! YEEEESSSSSS!'

I took my hands down from my face, sprang off my seat and ran over to throw my arms round my equally ecstatic father, celebrating Riquelme's penalty miss which had surely booked the place in our first ever Champions League final. Who we were to play was another question, as Barcelona held a slim 1-0 advantage over AC Milan, and no Arsenal fan wanted to face Puyol, Xavi and Co. But a goalless match at Camp Nou sent the Catalan champions through, and, suddenly, 17 May became the only date on the calendar I was interested in.

The days dragged by in school and work. Teachers were talking about the foundations of a good study plan for our upcoming GCSEs, but I could only daydream about team formations... would Campbell and Toure deal with Ronaldinho and Eto'o... would Henry step up to the plate in one of the biggest matches the team have ever played... and would my new-found faith in the questionable antics of one Jens Lehmann be maintained?

After we qualified from the group stages, I realised that I had worn the same Arsenal shirt and navy tracksuit bottoms for every match we'd won and decided this was no coincidence and my choice of clothes was obviously a good luck charm. On the day of the final, while I was studying for my first GCSE which was taking place the next day, my mum was ironing and let out a sudden gasp.

'Oh no, no...'

'What? What is it?'

'Nothing. It's nothing.'

'What did you do? Did you burn yourself?'

She hadn't burnt herself, but she had burnt an enormous hole in the knee of my tracksuit bottoms. I told myself it didn't mean anything. I would wear them anyway; surely the huge hole they now had didn't mean they were any less lucky... right?

After realising studying was pointless as nothing was sinking in because of my nerves, I started to decorate my living room with every Arsenal picture, poster, flag and scarf I could lay my hands on in my house (which was quite a lot). By kick-off, every wall in my living room was red and white from top to bottom and covered with famous faces, from Charlie George to Dennis Bergkamp. My entire family, including my mum, dad, four sisters and even a few cousins, squeezed into my house, and we took our seats. We were ready for one of the most important matches in our history.

Everything seemed to be going pretty evenly until the 18th minute when a typical sporadic outburst from Lehmann saw him run outside the box, foul Eto'o, get a straight red and ensure that Robert Pires left Arsenal in the worst way imaginable, having to be substituted for by the then rookie keeper Almunia. My faith in him was completely lost. Not only were we facing one of, if not the best, team in Europe, we were now doing it with 10 men.

Things were looking bleak, with Barcelona making the most of their one-man advantage, until a glimmer of hope came from an unlikely source as Sol Campbell jumped heroically to head Arsenal into the lead 10 minutes before halftime. I know I jumped and cheered, but everything was suddenly very fuzzy, and all I can remember is sitting with my head in my hands afterwards feeling dizzy and praying for halftime to come so the team and I could regroup and get over the shock lead.

The first half was painful; the second half was a million times worse. Every time Barcelona attacked, I flinched and turned away like I was watching a horror film, and I should have just turned the television off when Henry fired a shot that should have left the ball curling in the back of the net but instead went straight at Valdés. But the introduction of Larsson proved to be pivotal as the ex-Celtic Swede highlighted our one-man deficit. When Eto'o equalised with a goal set up by Larsson, my thoughts jumped to extra time and penalties. 1-1 wasn't the end of the world as long as we could hold on. Four minutes later, I knew it was over. Larsson's cross found Belletti, who slid the ball through Almunia's legs and into the back of the net. I felt like Belletti had jumped from the screen and kicked me right in the stomach, and as the minutes agonisingly went on and no equaliser was found, the final whistle brought tears and sheer disappointment. I'd seen my father cry once before: 17 May 2006. That night brought the total up to two.

The worst thing about football is that you never fully accept what happened and always ask: 'What if?' What if the referee had let Giuly's goal stand and just booked Lehmann, would we have come back? What if Henry had buried that chance he had in the second half? What if Larsson and Belletti had been left on the bench, would our name have finally gone onto the Champions League trophy? And what if we never get the chance to be in the final again and have to carry on listening to the taunts of Manchester United and Liverpool fans endlessly?

After the 2006 final, I think that when, not if, WHEN, Arsenal win the Champions League, I'll feel like I have personally lifted the trophy and celebrated with the team on behalf of every Arsenal fan who went through the same pain I experienced that night but still carry on supporting their team regardless; win, lose or draw.

Sarah Rooney *pictured with her dad on page 51*

A VERY SPECIAL FRIENDSHIP

My love affair with Arsenal Football Club started on 29 April 1950, watching the Cup Final against Liverpool on our 9" black and white PYE television set. I was hooked, though my first live match was not until 24 April 1954, the year after a record Championship win. The match was Arsenal versus Middlesbrough (3-1) and the start of 18 years with no success, not even the smell of a trophy. Recently, fans became increasingly impatient when the club didn't win a trophy for eight years...that was nothing, I can tell you!

The spell was broken on 28 April 1970—the European Fairs Cup win. What a night! Grown men crying! This was, of course, bettered the next season with the first Double. A nil-nil draw or a win would seal the Championship. Any other result would mean another year or more in the doldrums. This match against Spurs was, as you can imagine, particularly memorable. A friend and I left work early in good time for the 7.30pm kick-off. What an amazing sight at White Hart Lane, with thousands of fans queuing to get in. No all-ticket matches in those days. We patiently joined the queue and very slowly moved towards the entrance.

With kick-off fast approaching, we were agonisingly near. But the crowd in front of us were becoming impatient and started to surge forward. There was one policeman on horseback, but he was unable to control the crowd. Then, literally 20 yards from the entrance another sudden surge almost took us off our feet, and we were in danger of being crushed. We were scared and had to give up! The next couple of hours we wandered nervously around the streets together with hundreds of other fans listening and trying to judge what was happening by the OOOHs and AAAHs of the crowd who were lucky enough to be inside the stadium.

Time passed and still no sign of that special noise that would signify a goal. In those days, the gates were opened a few minutes from the end to allow fans to leave early if they so wished. Obviously, for this particular match, not many people were leaving early. My friend and I took this opportunity to quickly enter the ground and find a spot to watch the last few minutes. We arrived just a minute or so before Ray Kennedy scored. We were overjoyed but aware that a goal for Spurs would give the title to Leeds. Those last couple of minutes seemed to take ages to tick away. An almighty last assault on the Arsenal penalty area saw Bob Wilson smother and grab the ball safely. He kicks the ball downfield and the whistle blows! The title comes back to Highbury. I find it difficult to describe how I felt. After watching mediocre seasons for 18 years, at last, something to really cheer about. Tears and cheers! The police were rather more lenient in those days, and the fans were allowed on the pitch to hail their heroes. That's the first and last time that I have ever invaded a football pitch. And White Hart Lane at that. The icing on the cake—the FA Cup win just a few days later. The Arsenal fans, including me, were directly behind the goal when Charlie George scored. I have enjoyed many memorable moments in the following years—the victory at Anfield, more Doubles, a Cup Winners' Cup Final—but looking back, nothing compares with that night at White Hart Lane.

Many friendships were made as a result of following Arsenal, mainly through my interest in collecting Arsenal ephemera, such as programmes, books, cigarette cards, menus, newspapers and statistics. And not only friendships with Arsenal supporters but also supporters of other, mainly London, clubs. We would

have meetings and get-togethers in our homes or local hostelries as well as annual summer reunions around the London area. Concerning friendships, I must mention Roger Desouches, Peter Emmins, Lee Faust, Eddie Stubbings and Fred Ollier, the official Arsenal statistician from Crewe whose knowledge of anything Arsenal is phenomenal. However, this article is dedicated to my very special friendship with Arthur Booth *[pictured on page 54]*, who passed away in 1994 just after the Cup Winners' Cup win against Parma. For over 35 years, we had been watching the Gunners through highs and lows. The debacle against Swindon in 1969 and Leeds the year before. The Double as described previously. Travelling home from Wolves in a snowstorm (lost 1-5). Getting soaked on Arthur's scooter on the way to a match at West Ham. Trying to watch Gillingham versus Arsenal (League Cup) with fog and mist swirling around the ground. The West Ham match was interesting.

In 1959, before the days of European Club Championships, various minor competitions were arranged including the Southern Floodlight Cup between clubs in the South of England. Arsenal were playing West Ham in the semi-final. Mel Charles, the brother of the great John Charles, had just been signed by Arsenal with the hope that he would start a new era of success at Highbury. He was not eligible for league matches but could play in this competition. At that time, I had just started work in the same office as Arthur in the City of London. We soon discovered our joint love of football and of Arsenal FC in particular.

Arthur started giving me lifts to matches on his Vespa. For this match, we left the City after work in torrential rain. We had to stop on the Canning Town flyover to try and dry out before continuing our journey. The soaking proved worthwhile as Arsenal won 2-0, and Charles on his senior debut scored twice. We looked forward with hope to the future. Unfortunately, after a good start and a few goals, things didn't work out.

I think the millstone of his brother was too great, and he did not fulfill his early promise. Injuries did not help, and he was soon transferred to Cardiff. Arthur and I went from standing on the terraces in 1958 to being season ticket holders from 1972. There we sat for the next 22 years until his unfortunate illness and his untimely passing. He was and will be sorely missed and left a gap which still exists. He would have dearly loved the seasons since his passing with all that has transpired, such as the Wenger era, two further Doubles, Dennis Bergkamp and the Emirates Stadium.

Bernard Chaplin

A NORTH LONDON ODYSSEY

WHAT'S IN A NAME?

I was born in 1962 and brought up on a council estate in Liverpool called Cantril Farm, although locally it was known as Cannibal Farm. All the kids on the estate either supported Liverpool or Everton, but in truth, I was never really comfortable with either club, even though I towed the line during kickabouts on the estate. But then, on Cup Final day, Saturday 8 May 1971, when I was nine years old, my life was to change forever. On the morning of the Liverpool versus Arsenal match, all the local kids gathered to play our own version of the big match that was to follow at Wembley Stadium; there were about 18 of us, and we were split into two sides. As I was a goalie and on the Arsenal side, I ran off to take my position between the two jumpers, imagining I was actually Billy Mercer, and then it happened. As I turned round to face the teams, everyone was pointing at me, and they were all chanting: 'Arsenal! Arsenal! Arsenal!' And in that split second, my love affair with the Gunners was born, and my 'Arsenal' nickname stuck. In 1979, events took another unlikely turn following a bad accident. I was taken to hospital by friends, although the medical staff were slightly baffled as to why they had no records for an 'Arsenal Whittick' when they checked their files before treating me, so, shortly after I was discharged, I set about changing my name properly and officially by Deed Poll. Following Arsenal's 6-1 drubbing at Goodison Park in November 1985, I was walking back to my home reading the match programme when a man, who was just about to open his front gate as I passed, asked me what the score was. Instinctively I replied, 'We got beat 6-1 mate!' The man did not respond well to the information. 'You're ******* joking!' he exploded, and with that he slammed the front gate, stormed back across his garden and into his house, slamming that door behind him, too. I hope he didn't have a cat or a dog. I've often wondered when he eventually discovered that he'd asked the only Scouser in Liverpool who supported Arsenal the score! After growing up in Liverpool and being called Arsenal, I had to become one of the fastest runners in our playground, but watching on from the Anfield main stand as Michael Thomas clinched the title for Arsenal on that amazing Friday night in May 1989 made all the grief I had to put up with while growing up worthwhile!

Arsenal Whittick *pictured left at Highbury*

우린 죽을 때까지 아스날.

The writing that you can see above reads 'Arsenal 'til I Die' in Korean, and, as a dedicated Gooner, this is how I feel about our club. In the photograph, you can see me at the Emirates, which is famous around the whole world. This picture was taken a couple of years ago when I was at school in London, but now I am supporting from a distance of five and a half thousand miles away.

I see most games via television and shout and scream my support in both languages. When I was at Goodison Park for the first game of the 2009/10 season and Eduardo scored our sixth goal on 88 minutes, there I was shouting. And then switching back into English: 'Come on you reds, shoot the ball into the net. We want seven!'

I come from a household where my father is—wait for it—a Manchester United supporter! But never mind, I am working on it. When he is fast asleep and snoring like a giant sea whale, I creep into his room and whisper into his ear in English, 'Arsenal are the best! Arsenal are the best!' Or in Korean: 'Arsenalen chehgoyah!' One day soon he will wake up screaming, as the ghosts of his Man United support rise up to torment him. Anyway, my dad has already got the message because my entire bedroom is covered in posters of all of my heroes: Fàbregas, Arshavin, Walcott, van Persie. Maybe that's why he's not been in there for so long!

My mum is different, though. I've taken her to the Emirates a number of times, and she now jumps up with excitement every time we score. So I know her loyalties lie in the right place.

Not many Arsenal fans know it, but we have a very big following over here in Korea with a special official website to keep us up-to-date called Arsenal.Korea, which attracts thousands of hits each day.

[Left] Pictured in his
Arsenal-themed bedroom
and [previous page] at the
Emirates

This special website has translated the English version into a Korean version. However, many of us fans don't just rely upon the official website. Some of us supporters make our own blogs to support Arsenal, exchanging information on transfers, schedules, the uniqueness of each player and reviews. I am part of a widespread Arsenal community around Korea who daily surf this website and blogs.

English Arsenal supporters would be surprised to learn about how much Korean youth know of the Barclays Premier League. Many children know the teams and the players. In response to this huge interest, special video games and highlights programmes directed towards the younger generation have been developed.

I was lucky enough to see most of the games we played during the 2008/09 FA Youth Cup run, and, although we eventually won the trophy very convincingly, the highlight was surely the game at White Hart Lane when our players including Jay Emmanuel-Thomas, Jack Wilshire and Sanchez Watt really imposed themselves onto a fancied and fairly talented Spurs team. With nearly 25,000 in the stadium, you could feel the silence of the Spurs fans as our boys gave them a football masterclass throughout the second half. We had about 3,000 fans and made a lot more noise than the others. The importance of this run of games was that we fans got to see what Arsène Wenger has been building for our future. In a couple more seasons, there will be a new group of home-grown players coming into the first team, ready to challenge everyone. We got a glimpse into the future and, believe it or not, in a couple of years' time, in thousands of boys' bedrooms all over Korea, there will be posters of these new young Arsenal stars! I can't wait to be back in London soon to enjoy that special feeling of being at the Emirates with 60,000 people who feel just like me.

Yongbeom Kim

ARSENAL BOUND US TOGETHER

Imagine having a father who not only went to Highbury during the Golden Era of the 1930s, thus witnessing Arsenal's legendary all-conquering team, but who also was on good terms with quite a few of those players, too! I was born in 1947 into a totally pro-Arsenal family, living a couple of miles from the ground, and brought up on tales from that amazing pre-war era. However, my formative years weren't anywhere near as glorious, and I found myself growing up in one of those dreadful fallow periods that have occasionally affected our beloved club.

Admittedly, we won the league in 1948 and 1953, but you wouldn't believe me if I told you I remembered anything from the first campaign, and the sad truth is I have no memory of the second—although, I think it was the excitement in my home that led to demands on my part to be actually taken to a game. Initially my father resisted, claiming, 'You'll be running around before half-time', but agreed to take me to a match at White Hart Lane instead, not to see Tottenham, mind you, but for an Amateur Cup tie between Wood Green Town and Dulwich Hamlet.

My father *[pictured above with Tony as a child and with his car]* eventually relented in 1955, though, and started taking me to reserve matches at Highbury in front of crowds of around 7,000—more when we played a London team—and I endured his stories from days gone by. Of course, there is nothing kids hate

more than tales from yesteryear, especially as it became obvious, even to my young eyes, that from the moment I started watching Arsenal, the club stopped winning the big trophies.

But my father, despite having no connection with the club other than being a supporter, knew some of the stars through owning a garage and car repair yard in Westbury Avenue off Turnpike Lane. Some of the players and ex-players came in for petro l, to have repairs done or, in a few cases, to house the cars overnight. So, I heard stories, and yet more stories. I even met one or two of the players at the garage, and they patted me on the head and ruffled my hair. Now, you have to appreciate that my relating of

these stories today comes 50 years after I heard the tales, and my father was, in many cases, telling me his reminiscences 25 years after they happened. And that leads us to the nature of oral history—you can never be quite sure what's what.

My father was born in 1910 (coincidentally the year Norris took over Woolwich Arsenal), and he told me that my grandfather had actually gone to Highbury in the 1913/14 season—the first year at the new ground. My grandfather was a splendid gent who owned a piano factory in Stoke Newington and who, in my memory, always wore a three-piece suit and a watch chain, and I always remember him being kind and loving towards me, but he was not a man who got down on his knees to play with his grandson. So I never got to talk to him much about the Arsenal, although he always asked me if I'd been that week, who I had seen and how they were doing.

So I never asked him if he had been to Highbury in 1913/14, but he did tell me that in his day, Highbury had been 'a right mess', holding 20,000 or so most of the time. I remember the phrase 'a right mess', and I think that reflected the fact that before the war the ground simply wasn't finished.

I do also remember my grandfather speaking of the Os and still calling them Clapton (in the way that older folk sometimes hold onto old names). I think Clapton was the team he went to see before Arsenal appeared in North London in 1913, and, as soon as Arsenal were there, they switched allegiance, not least because Highbury was closer to Stoke Newington than Clapton (Tottenham were never an option). Since the factory worked on Saturday mornings, it made getting to the ground in the afternoon easier—especially in the winter when games kicked off at 2.15pm. If my recollections of conversations with my grandfather as a young teenager are correct, then he went to the first Arsenal versus Clapton Orient game at Highbury on 18 April 1913. The crowd was a record-breaking 35,000.

As for my father, he was certainly going to Highbury by the time he left City of London School aged about 16 (the family didn't have the funds to send him to university), which means he was there within a year of the start of the Chapman era.

Now this is going to sound like utter sacrilege, but my father told me later that 'Chapman wasn't that good!' His view was that he was good at Huddersfield but didn't have it at Arsenal. I'd like to say otherwise, but that's what I remember. From what I was told, there was a real expectation that when Chapman arrived, Arsenal would finally win something. It took a while, and people got dispirited and disconsolate.

By the 1930s, however, my father had broken away from the City, where he had worked as a clerk and had limited opportunities to go to the football. By 1935, he set up his own business, a car breakers yard in Westbury Avenue. He was also by that time playing piano and saxophone in a dance band, and it is this period—1935 until the outbreak of war—that was the source of many of his stories.

My father would go to matches not with pals (he was not a teetotaller, but he never had much taste for the booze and the football was then, as now, something one did to the accompaniment of beer) but more often than not with people who were his customers at the car breakers. (Cars, I should explain, were endlessly built and rebuilt in those days. You took the bits that worked out of one car and managed somehow to fix them into position in another, generally of a different make. Forget digital—this wasn't even analogue. It was patch-and-mend technology, using whatever came to hand.)

He told me how he took one customer to a game played on a pitch that was a mud bath. Ted Drake was playing and playing tirelessly, according to my dad, trying to deliver and get onto passes that just got stuck in the morass. My father's colleague spent the game shouting at Drake to 'get a bloody move on' and 'stop hanging around'. My father was outraged and would have told the man what for, but he wanted to keep the car-repairing contract.

It's an interesting little thought: the way some 'fans' dish out negative treatment and groans is not a modern phenomena. I got many stories about how some disenchanted Arsenal fans complained that even when winning the league we did not win every match.

My father really did have a soft spot for Ted Drake and mentioned him once scoring four in a game that was so one-sided Arsenal virtually stopped playing in the second half to avoid embarrassing the opposition. From what I can recall, I think this was Arsenal 8, Middlesbrough 0 in April 1935, on the way to the third successive league win.

I did ask my father, as a teenager, if the dislike of Tottenham was as strong then as now, and he said it certainly was. The flat I was brought up in, on Devonshire Hill Lane, had my Arsenal family on the first floor and a Tottenham family on the floor below. I can remember my mother saying once: 'Don't let them talk about football!' There was a worry the men would really get angry. But mostly when my father thought back to the 1930s, his view was that in those days Tottenham didn't matter—maybe a reflection of the fact that in 1934/35, when Arsenal won the league, Tottenham ended up bottom of the table and were relegated. My dad certainly claimed he remembers the time 'we put six past them', but I think on that one his memory was playing up. That season we beat them 5-1 (hat-trick for Drake, 70,000 in the stadium).

As I mentioned, during this period my father supplemented his income as a car breaker by playing piano, and later saxophone, in a dance band. He told me that as the band was made up of Arsenal men, when they could, they'd get bookings in the towns where Arsenal were playing. They'd leave London, often early on Saturday morning, so as to be able to drive through the town in an open-top car on the Saturday lunchtime, waving at bemused locals, as if they were the Arsenal team (playing for the Arsenal made you much more famous than being a film star in the 30s). Then they placed their instruments in the dance hall, drove off to the match, watched Arsenal knock hell out of Leicester, Derby, Birmingham or whoever it was, and then go back to the dance hall to earn their money. I gather that very few people went to away games in those days, so they certainly stood out in the game.

I think it was one of the times when he was at his happiest (he'd also just started dating my mum). I don't have any pictures of my father at Highbury (cameras were used mostly on holiday in those days), but I have got two wonderful publicity shots of the band, which gives the feel of the gang and the era.

I know they were in Portsmouth on Christmas Eve 1938, because one of my early memories of an away match with my parents was 20 years later (6 December 1958), when Arsenal won at Fratton Park 1-0, Gordon Nutt scoring. As my parents and I drove into the city, we saw a big banner up across a main street reading 'Portsmouth Welcome Arsenal'. My dad spent much of the day telling us both that the last time he was there, they played at a particular dance hall (which he suggested we go and find, although he was dissuaded by my mother and me). He said it had been freezing cold and a terrible match. I just looked it up. 0-0. Eddie Hapgood, Jack Crayson, Bernard Joy... On this occasion the memory can be verified. Christmas Eve, 1938.

I don't think supporters ever sang in those days, nor did they chant much (I might be wrong, but I am sure my father said that what we experienced later was 'not like the old days'). But if he and my grandfather were to be believed, what they did have was a huge amount of ref-baiting—that seemed to be the main sport. In an era of respect for officialdom, when a policeman could clip a teenager around the ear and send him on his way, shouting 'Where's your glasses, ref?' was the height of daring and seemed to cause much amusement. It all seems so tame to us now, but I was given tales of a spectator behind my father shouting, 'Come on, Arsenal, we want two points', and my father's friend replying, 'They're playing as if they've just had two pints!' That oft-repeated line always got a chuckle. Yes, there was probably some swearing in the ground, but it was muted and controlled.

Strangely, I also get the feeling that winning didn't matter so much as now. Of course, that might be because Arsenal were so good in the 1930s that any season when we didn't win the league was excused as a time for 'letting one of the other teams have a chance' (I certainly heard that phrase). But really it was more that going to The Arsenal was the thing to do. It was a time to have some fun with your mates—a bit like going to a dance. If we won, great, but if not, well... it didn't matter too much because North London had a team—a team that could take on anyone—and that had never happened before.

Which leads me on to the club's name. I am certain my grandfather called us Woolwich Arsenal sometimes, although our family was totally North London and so would never have gone to the Manor Ground. My father called us 'The Arsenal', as I think most of the generation that went as young men in the 30s did. It wasn't until he had retired and moved to Dorset in the 1960s that we were firmly 'Arsenal'.

After the war, my father married—I was born in 1947—but he still went to football on Saturday afternoons, and it was in the 1950s as a youth occasionally taken along to my father's garage (no longer breaking cars, but instead selling petrol and replacing batteries) that I was introduced to... well, who? 'Son...' (he often called me 'Son'), 'This is... XXX—he played for Arsenal', and I would dutifully shake hands in that way that little boys do, not quite sure how to handle the situation.

But, I am so sorry to say, I can't remember the names, and I never thought to get an autograph, nor to ask my dad much later, 'Who were those Arsenal players who came to the garage?' To me as a child, they were just old men (you know what it is like for children—everyone is old). Memory is strange; odd items stick in your mind, and you can become certain of them, but then you check some detail and find it is not all true. Yet there's one from a little later that is so clear, I am sure it was true. It is almost as if I watched it happen yesterday.

We lived, as I have mentioned, in our flat off Devonshire Hill Lane. I recall having been to school and getting very muddy playing football, or maybe just from mucking about on the way home. 'Mucking about'—it's what the kids used to do on the way home from school (home was tiny, and there was no TV, so mucking about was certainly preferable).

On seeing my state, my mum ordered me into the bath tub (no showers in post-war, jerry-built North London flats), and that is where I was when my dad came home from an afternoon match at Highbury. Afternoon, because they were playing Villa, and Villa didn't have floodlights at their ground, and so they always demanded that floodlights were not used when they played away.

'What was the score?' I demanded as dad came in to see me.

'4-0 to The Arsenal', he said. 'Any penalities?' 'No.' 'Anyone carried off injured?' 'No.' 'Anyone sent off for fighting?' 'No.' 'Not a very good game, then!' I decided. 'Actually, it was brilliant', he said.

Is this conversation a false memory? Who knows. But I do know that on 2 October 1957 Arsenal beat Villa 4-0 in front of what was for Highbury a tiny crowd of 18,000. Tiny because... yes, they kicked off at 2.30pm. Swallow, Tiddy, Bloomfield and Herd were the scorers, leaving Arsenal well placed with six wins, two defeats and a draw from the opening matches. It didn't last; the glory days were long gone, and we ended the season 12th, with a certain J Crayston as manager. But for reasons that will never become clear to me, that one moment stands out like a beacon. My dad coming home and reporting Arsenal had won 4-0.

Arsenal bound my father and me together. As I went through my teenage rebellion years (I was a teenager in the 1960s, after all), we fell out far more than we fell in. Of course later I deeply regretted the rows and arguments, and now the old man is gone, how I desperately want to turn the clock back and undo the shouting and stomping out (he never could understand my desire to have hair that went over my ears). But in truth, our lives together were endlessly saved and reunited by Arsenal, because no matter what, if we could go to Arsenal together, then everything would be repaired. My dad and I kept going to games together (although of course not all of them), even after he retired and we all moved to Dorset, and when I finally left home, I naturally returned to London.

Filming
*The Arsenal
Stadium Mystery*

Except that soon after I was offered a job in Algiers. My chance to go and see the world, and I took it. It was the summer of 1970. And you know what happened. I had supported Arsenal from childhood, but had no recollection of them winning anything, and then on the one occasion when they won everything, I was forced to follow the events on BBC World Service on short wave. The first great triumph for years, and I was on another continent. I did, however, manage to watch the Cup Final on Algerian TV at a friend's house. A lifetime of hearing about the great Gunners of the 1930s, and when finally the team get it together to win the Double, what happens? My father, still in England, going to watch the games, while I teach English to airline pilots in Africa! Of course, I've had my moments since and have seen the winning teams through the Graham and Wenger eras, so I have been singularly fortunate. But I think because of my time with my father at the ground, I've never lost my sense of proportion nor my sense of the history of Arsenal. As I mentioned, my father is no longer with us, but since he died, I've had a continuing desire somehow to commemorate what he saw—and indeed what my grandfather saw in the early days at Highbury. I think it was this notion of being born into an Arsenal family that was apparently at Highbury in the 1913/14 season that led me to start work on a book about Arsenal leading up to that era: *Making the Arsenal*, which came out in 2009. It tells the story of the collapse of Woolwich Arsenal and its takeover by Henry Norris in 1910 which the club kindly featured in the official prgramme.

For me, the point about the book is that I somehow wanted to relate it to football as my father and grandfather told it to me. Not just a set of facts about Norris' attempt to merge Arsenal with Fulham, but something that caught the passion and interest as it could be appreciated from a fan's point of view. So I wrote the book, not as a history, but as a novel—only the second novel ever on Arsenal (the first was *The Arsenal Stadium Mystery*, which became a film).

The joke in my family and among my friends is that if anyone suggests we play Trivial Pursuit, I ask if we can play the 1910 edition, because I know more about that era than the present day, and, indeed, I find myself rather bemused as to why I have become so totally fascinated with Arsenal's early times.

I grew up with Arsenal—with stories of the 1930s, told to me by my father and grandfather, who had seen their local team become the most talked about club in the world. Telling such stories in that way seems to me to be a really positive way to have history recorded. It is, after all, about the people and the interpretation, as much as it is about the facts.

Tony Attwood

ALL ABOARD

It all comes down to a single bus ride—the reason for being an Arsenal supporter and fan, that is! I have followed Arsenal since a fateful day near the beginning of the 1980/81 season; I was 13 years old, and my friend's older brother asked if we wanted to go to a football match. Now, there is much about this day and my introduction to Arsenal that has been forgotten. What I do know is the importance of that day to my life, the intervention of fate, and the magic is still very much alive and fresh within me to this day.

Before fate took a kind grasp of me and steered my life onto a new path, the game of football was of little interest. I knew it existed and had probably walked past a Cup game on TV, but I came from a family that had no interest in the sport. As such, I was not guided or taught about the importance of supporting one's club; I was not instilled with the magic and passion that existed. It is not hard to understand this, as I was part of a single parent family with two sisters, and at school I was not good at sports and terrible at kicking a ball. I was one of the last picked in any team, I suffered from asthma and my friends rarely played football at playtime, so football was not in my life.

What I do remember about the day that changed my life is getting to Finsbury Park, walking to Highbury, the first view of the East Stand and Arsenal's colours, the streets full of people. I remember having to enter the stadium via the kids' entrance, then the scrum, the pushing and shoving to get through a single gate in a fence that separated the kids' area and the North Bank, the terrace with everyone standing. We took our place near one of the barrier hoops behind the goal, and, as the crowd surged forward, my friend and I would duck under that hoop to not get squashed. The game and the teams are harder to remember. The players were unknown to me, but names such as Jennings, Sansom and O'Leary would soon fill my vocabulary; the skills and play on the pitch catch my imagination. The love of this game was taking hold, the people around, the songs that were sung, the friendship from strangers. The passion for the club radiated out, I was part of it and I did not want it to end. I had taken that first step to being a fan. Arsenal, My Arsenal: I had been found and taken into the fold. I belonged. The feeling was fantastic and is still with me to this day.

It all came down to a bus ride, a fateful bus journey, a journey that I am still on today even if the route is different, a journey of passion and love. What you need to know is that I grew up in Muswell Hill, and on that day in 1980, we all travelled to the ground on a bus. Muswell Hill Broadway is a roundabout with a bus depot in its centre, and two buses leave that depot and head down the steep side of Muswell Hill, and I thankfully climb aboard a W7 bus. I now have the knowledge to look back at fate, to look on that day and think what could have been, what might have been, how lucky I was to be on the W7. For the bus I sat on and looked out of the window from in excitement headed down Muswell Hill and past Park Road Swimming Pool, through and over Crouch End, before terminating a short walk from the stadium at Finsbury Park Bus Station. For that bus was the best bus I have ever sat on.

The other bus that starts its journey from the same place, the bus that could deal an innocent child a much different fate, a bus that could take you down a very different path, also gets driven down Muswell Hill on the same road, but for this bus a different route awaits it at the bottom of that steep, steep hill and, like the different path that I would have to lead, this other bus turns left and heads in a different direction to a different destination. The destination and a whole different fate is clearly shown on the front of the other bus and it is in big white letters: the sign says you are on a ONE FOUR FOUR bus and the destination is Tottenham.

I always look back on that day, even now, 30 years later as a season ticket holder, and I still get that buzz, that excitement, and I still get the goosebumps when I walk to every game. I thank my lucky stars for the bus with the W7 and the route to Finsbury Park; I thank my lucky stars that I said yes that day, that I walked with my friends to a football ground that I would come to love, a place called 'Highbury', and now the same route takes me and my family to Arsenal's new home, a stadium that is stunning, a testament to Arsenal, a place called 'Emirates', for this is all still in Finsbury Park and the area is the home of the greatest football club in the world. It is and will always be a proud place, a place where glory is important, where to strive for success is at its heart, 'Victory through Harmony', a place where my support will never cease, for me it will always be Arsenal 'til I die.

My son, Jake, has had a much different upbringing and has had football in his life since he was born. He came home from the hospital at a few days old just in time for the start of the 2002 World Cup. The Arsenal baton was handed down to him by the age of four. Arsenal was in his blood, and Jake had already attended his first games at Emirates. Jake sat on my lap the first time, and, as the ball passed, he read out the Arsenal players' shirt numbers, and I told him their names. Jake comes to most games with my wife and me, and he now knows all the players off by heart and has that belief that Arsenal can win everything. It's great for him to have the same hopes and dreams that I have carried with me from that fateful day 30 years ago.

Shaun Fuller *pictured with his family*

FIRST NAME TERMS

School holidays in the late 1950s and early 1960s were times for hanging about outside the main entrance at Highbury. A group of us lads from a mix of local primary schools would gather regularly and became Arsenal friends rather than neighbourhood or school friends. We knew every nook and cranny of the stadium, especially how to get in without paying. There was a very special turnstile by the corner of Avenell and Gillespie roads where the welding of the horizontal bars had been set just an inch too high in one place. This minor difference allowed some of us to squeeze through after the whistle had blown and scurry up the steps and into the massed legs of the crowd. When we did this, we were always seen by a very stern-looking, uniformed club official, but he would wink at us and flick his finger in the direction of the steps when it was all clear so we could get in. Once in, we would scramble through the massed legs, almost like cutting a way through the undergrowth in a jungle. I would get to the very front by the corner where there was a box which was used at halftime to put up the scores from other matches. The top of the box was covered with barbed wire, but who cared? I would sit on the top with a wonderful, clear view. No one ever asked me to get off.

One day in 1962, I met the most famous face in English football, Billy Wright, as he arrived to take charge of the club. He was always friendly towards us boys, and, although he might have given us his autograph several times already, he always repeated the gesture when asked. My proudest moment came one day when a very posh car came up and parked outside the main entrance. A man jumped out and opened the back door. Billy Wright came out from the other side of the front and his wife Joy, one of the famous Beverly sisters, stepped out onto the pavement. We boys were star-struck as she was the nearest thing to royalty any of us had ever seen. In those days, the pinnacle of fame was to have appeared at the London Palladium, and the Beverly sisters were regulars! And then Billy came straight towards me, holding Joy's hand, and said, 'Hello, Steven. Can I introduce my wife, Joy. I'm showing her round the place today.' Me, from the Ambler Road Primary School football team, introduced to one of the Beverly sisters by Billy Wright. Such Highbury moments stay with you forever.

Steve Cowan

ARSENAL
"THE GUNNERS"
Arsenal Stadium
London

SAMMY TO THE RESCUE

As a young boy, I used to stand behind the goal at the Clock End, and, as I lived a short 15-minute walk away from Highbury, often arriving at about five to three, my friends and I were often passed, hand-to-hand, over the heads of supporters from the stairs near the turnstiles, right to the front row by the touchline. Even as late as the 1960s, people cared enough about young kids being able to see and would gladly help them to get down to the front. Because I stood in the same place every week, I slowly got on nodding terms with most of the fans who surrounded me, and I particularly remember a group of young Turkish blokes who were extremely passionate Arsenal men who all wore red and white scarves and sang very loudly. One evening in 1979, Arsenal were playing Fenerbahce at home in the Cup Winners' Cup. I couldn't believe my eyes when I took my place behind the goal; the Turkish guys were all wearing Turkish or Fenerbahce colours, and, although they got a lot of teasing from the regulars all around, there was no hint of trouble, and they still cheered and jumped up and down when Arsenal scored their two goals through Alan Sunderland and Willie Young—those lads couldn't lose that night!

At school, I was as good as gold and never in any trouble; however, supporting Arsenal was a passion, and on two occasions, I have to admit to having bunked off. The first time was to watch a Cup replay against Derby County, which was played one February afternoon in 1972 during the miners' strike, and, because of the threat of power cuts, the FA decided that the match should be played during daylight to avoid any backlogs in fixtures.

There was a massive crowd of over 63,000 that day, so many in fact that a crush barrier failed, and some people were injured. I remember the incident for two reasons: Firstly, it happened very close to where I

was standing in the Clock End, but mostly because the press photographers were taking lots of photos of the scene, and I was supposed to be at school. I was terrified of being snapped at the game and a teacher seeing my photo in the paper or on TV! I was so concerned that I crouched down and kept my head out of sight. Looking back at the whole incident, it was extremely scary, especially with so many people in the crowd getting hurt, but I have to admit that at that age, I was just happy getting away with being off school and watching my Arsenal.

The second time I skipped off school that season was to get a good position in the queue to buy my FA Cup semi-final tickets, and not going to lessons that day meant I was able to get there early enough to get a place in the first 100 or so fans. Lucky that I did, too, as just half an hour or so later, the line of people stretched right up Avenell Road and along by the flats at the top of the hill as far as I could see. But despite being so early, for some strange reason when I arrived at the ground for the semi, I discovered the ticket I had been sold was in the Sunderland end. I was a lone 14-year-old Arsenal fan, kitted out in my Arsenal scarf, among an army of Mackems. Thankfully, the Sunderland fans were all very good to me, and I got chatting to a fair few of them. Then, without any warning, a particularly large Sunderland fan picked me up and made me stand on the top of the barrier in front of him, while he and all his mates propped me up, told me to raise my scarf above my head and that if I didn't start singing 'You'll Never Walk Alone', they wouldn't let me down. I felt really embarrassed as I was hoisted up and clearly worried and concerned about how the other Sunderland fans would react, but I did as they insisted and nervously sang the song with my arms raised holding my Arsenal scarf. To my surprise and definite relief, I got a round of applause that seemed to come from all round me, but more importantly my 'mates' were good to their word and let me down. Sunderland then scored what turned out to be the winning goal, and, because none of the Sunderland fans had ever been to a Cup Final before, their nervous tension leading up to the final whistle was unbelievable. Although I was fed up and disappointed by the result, I wished them luck for Wembley. That was the day I discovered that real football fans are all the same, part of one big family, regardless of

who they support.

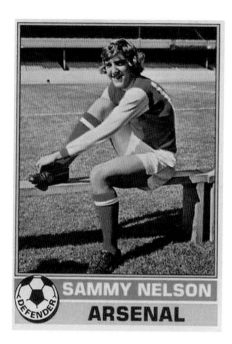

SAMMY NELSON
DEFENDER
ARSENAL

In 1980, I took on a paper round, and one of the houses I delivered newspapers to was where the Arsenal left-back Sammy Nelson lived. I didn't see him often because I delivered the papers very early, but I'll never forget the morning of the Arsenal versus West Ham final. At about 10am, I got a phone call from the paper shop owner to tell me that Sammy had popped in the night before and dropped off two tickets to give to the lad who delivered his papers. I was thrilled to bits, and my girlfriend and I rushed off to Wembley and just about made it in time for kick-off. We didn't care that we had to stand right at the back. Although, sadly, we lost the game 1-0, I'll never forget that generous and thoughtful gesture by my former Arsenal hero and will always be grateful to have been supporting the club during an era when the players genuinely had a connection with the supporters and cared enough to go out of their way ahead of a massively important game to help a fan like me. Arsenal 'til I die.

Paul Reynolds

PICCADILLY LINE LOVERS

As an Arsenal fan, I was delighted to get a temporary hospitality job at Emirates Stadium a few seasons ago. After the Gunners had beaten Manchester City one night, I finished my shift at 11pm and rushed to get to Holloway Road Tube station. I was exhausted and looking forward to getting home when three men got on the Tube, too, and sat opposite me. They had been to the match and had clearly been celebrating the win. We chatted a bit, but I was tired and worried about missing my train at Victoria station. When I changed from the Piccadilly Line to the Victoria Line and King's Cross, I noticed them following me, but thought it was just a coincidence that they were travelling in the same direction. When I reached Victoria station, I ran to get the last train to Bromley, but found it weird as they were running for the same train! We talked a bit more, but they were drunk and loud, apart from Phil, the quiet one, who offered to walk me home as it was very late when we finally reached Bromley station. I would never usually trust someone I'd just met, but something seemed different, and I wanted to get to know Phil. As he walked me home, we chatted, although mainly about our love of football. It turned out that he lived nearby, so we swapped numbers and decided to meet up. After our first date, which was a night of non-stop chatting and laughing, we soon became a couple. Then, two years later, we got married. So, whenever we watch a game at the Emirates, we always think back to that fateful evening that we met on the Tube and, thanks to our love for Arsenal, our lives were brought together.

Atiyah Meadows *pictured with Phil*

I'M FOREVER INDEBTED TO ARSENAL

There are moments in your life that stay with you forever—moments where you can feel your life changing, moments where you commit your mind and also your heart. Over the course of my life so far there are many moments that have left their imprint on me: from debilitating, emotional pain to joy capable of erasing any heartache or loss. The day my girlfriend passed away. The moment I moved into my very own apartment. My first dog, Rusky, a mixed pedigree that I obtained in exchange for a bag of dog pellets. I loved him dearly; he was my much-needed best friend at a time when I felt alone as a child. I also remember the moment that I fell madly in love with a girl, but she didn't even know my name. I also remember the moment that Arsenal became a part of my life forever and became a part of me. I will forever be indebted to Arsenal Football Club for the hours of joy (and even the disappointment) they have brought into my life. Yes, we could do with more trophies and have come agonisingly close on too many occasions, but hope springs eternal, and next season the fans will all unite once again and do so every year until glory is ours to enjoy once again!

Tim Sylvester

ARSENAL BOUND US TOGETHER

Arsenal versus Tottenham—my first ever North London derby, and I remember it all so well. My dad and I sat behind Paul Robinson's goal and exchanged so much banter with the Spurs fans that afternoon. Emmanuel Adebayor scored just after halftime, at my end, although Dimitar Berbatov scored an equaliser pretty quickly afterwards, and then Robbie Keane had a penalty saved by Manuel Almunia. The atmosphere was amazing; I'd never heard the Emirates as loud! Then Bendtner came on for Eboue just before a corner, and the guy sitting next to us, who had annoyed both of us all afternoon with his dumb comments and who my dad and I had decided was a classic once-a-season 'armchair merchant', said, 'Nik's gonna score with his first touch!' I just looked at him, with one of those looks, and laughed. 'No chance', I thought. The next thing I saw was Nicklas Bendtner flying towards the ball and heading it past the Spurs keeper, just as my new 'armchair' friend jumped on top of my dad and me—all three of us screaming like babies and hugging like lifelong buddies. The Gunners held out for the win, and, as we left the ground to get the Tube afterwards, my dad took us the wrong way back to the Tube station, down St Thomas Road with all the Tottenham fans, just us two in our Arsenal shirts standing out like sore thumbs. Did I care? Arsenal just beat Tottenham three days before Christmas—of course I didn't!

Joe Hurd *pictured with his dad*

WALKING ON WATER

Watching the World Cup always brings out the romantic in me and makes me think of all the greats that I am too young to have seen play—the type of players who, I feel, are better than almost any of their contemporaries—Pele, Alfredo di Stefano, Zico, Bobby Charlton, Franz Beckenbauer, Liam Brady, Johnny Giles, Ferenc Puskas, Gianni Rivera, George Best and Teofilo Cubillas, to name just a few. In my head, they are perhaps twice as good as they actually were on the field, but I still feel like I have missed out on something, and the grainy footage that plays on my DVD player doesn't really do the players justice. But last night, after watching Germany demolish a static Australia at South Africa 2010, I sat down and, instead of pining to 'have seen Brady play at Highbury just once', I actually thought how lucky I was to have seen some of the players I have seen over the years.

I was born in 1986, got caught up in the football fever that swept Ireland during Italia 90, before becoming a Gooner in 1994. During that time, I've seen some wonderful players: Maradona still had a bit left in his legs during the early 90s, and there was that wonderful AC Milan team of Rossi, Baresi, Maldini, Rijkaard and Weah, and the insane skills of Zidane, Raul, Ronaldinho and Ronaldo (the Brazilian one) in their prime. And, as Arsenal fans, we have been extremely fortunate in that we've had some players who were often in a league of their own on the field, and, in my eyes, one stands head and shoulders above the rest: the Iceman, DB10!

Dennis Bergkamp's arrival in London in 1995 saw the beginning of a new dawn at Arsenal as the club began to look to Europe for more talent, although the Dutchman came to us under a cloud. At the time, Dennis was the second most expensive signing in the world after Inter Milan paid Ajax £12m for his services in 1993. He flattered to deceive in Italy and, just two years on, he arrived in North London for £7.5m. During the very early days, many claimed that Arsenal had wasted what was then a decent sum of money. Now it is seen as one of the biggest bargains in football history. It took Bergkamp seven games to score his first goal for the Gunners (against Southampton), and during this time, he went through a tough transitional period, but when he got going, boy did he get going! There was literally no stopping him.

In 423 games, he scored 120 goals, and I have enough confidence to say that NOT ONE of them were run-of-the-mill tap-ins. Bergkamp didn't do run-of-the-mill, he did majestic, he did magical, he did genius. I have studied English Literature in college, read the greats like Byron, Keats, Shakespeare and Joyce, yet I still struggle to find a superlative to do justice to the Iceman. Just talking about some of Bergkamp's goals is akin to talking about Michael Jackson's dancing—they were merely the icing on the proverbial cake. Michael Jackson was much more than a talented dancer—he was a songwriter, a singer, an entertainer, even the king. Likewise, Bergkamp was more than a goalscorer—he was the songwriter, singer and entertainer in our pack. Some of the passes he tried were ridiculous. To even think of attempting these passes was breath-taking, but he could actually carry them off. Dennis also created goals, lots of goals, and found space for team-mates so they could excel, too. And for 11 years, ELEVEN YEARS, it was Arsenal fans and Arsenal Football Club who benefited from his genius. It was US who got to watch him week in, week out, while every manager in Europe wished they'd taken a punt on the man who nobody seemed to want when he was in Italy. Nobody else got him after us, either; we had Bergkamp's wonder all to ourselves, and never, ever forget just how lucky we were to see that.

Dream of Puskas, Pele and Maradona, wonder now at Messi, Kaka and perhaps Torres, but remember that once upon a time everyone else was doing the wishing. Dennis Bergkamp was the most technically gifted player to ever ply his trade in English football, and he did so at the home of football. Some say his career was marred by the fact he wouldn't fly and thus missed out on some vital European games, but let me conclude by asking a simple question: Would you fly if you could walk on water?

Mary O'Shea

THE BEAUTIFUL GAME

My sons and I waited six years to get our season tickets for the Arsenal and were finally lucky for the second season at the Emirates. Every home match day I awake with the same feeling of excitement I had when going to the occasional game as a red member! It doesn't matter how the team has performed in the last match, home or away, the fans approach each game with renewed optimism and faith. I love the buzz as we cross the bridge to the stadium, surrounded by this optimism in anticipation of a great performance. We have become more familiar with our fellow season ticket neighbours as the seasons roll on. Recently, the team put us through 92 minutes of stress until, eureka, 'Super Nick' headed home a winner against Wolves in the 93rd minute. Much hugging with my sons followed that goal, but also with one of our fellow supporters! Where else would you hug a complete stranger, other than when sharing joy at your team's success? The beautiful, beautiful game played the Arsenal way!

Debbie Freeland *pictured with her sons*

THE FINAL SACRIFICE

I glanced up at my dad as he looked on at Roberto Carlos and Zidane sharing a private joke on the velvet green Highbury turf. A wry smile swept across his face a Robinho and Beckham rifled in shots awash a backdrop of red and white. Could we possibly add a fairytale ending to the heroics at the Bernabeu? Glancing around at the faces in the crowd, it seemed everyone bore the same expression. If Henry really was to be convinced Arsenal was his home, he would need our 12th man more than ever.

Highbury rocked that night and seemed to shift the goalposts in Arsenal's favour as Raul bore down on goal. The fans had forgotten all about those names that graced the opposition's team sheet; it was the Arsenal name that would go up in lights that night. Two days later and back to reality when the phone rings. We had tickets. Again. The same enticing smile crossed my dad's face. 'Are you sure you want to put yourself through all that again?' was his sarcastic remark. 'And miss us win?' I jovially responded.

A changing of the guard happened that night. Fàbregas would replace Vieira in the hearts of all Arsenal fans and the cheers would go up as Juventus' players fell short of the scintillating London club's style. From that moment, superstition played on the mindsets of father and son. We just had to watch all the games together from now on. It was a winning formula.

Again the anxious wait by the phone to see if we were to continue our own Champions League run, never mind that of the Arsenal itself. Smoke billowing from burger vans and the introduction of bright yellow among the familiar red and white of the fans revealed that our journey was not to end just yet. At one point, my dad was nearly swept aside by a swarm of these Spanish invaders to Highbury, only to regain his balance and composure once again. It was to be a foreboding sign for the tie ahead. How we needed Toure's goal.

Little did we realise just how important the actions of an erratic German would be in Spain. Just like the submarine emblem of Villarreal, Arsenal's run in Europe seemed to be going under. But Mad Jens had understood that, in a small house in England, a father and son had watched the game together, his lucky charm. So Paris laid in wait and more importantly the Catalan giants. Forget the Eiffel Tower, I thought, we have our own global icon in Henry and the now deadly duo of my father and me. The phone rang:

'I am really sorry, I only have one ticket for the final!' Time stopped. How could I let my dad, who had supported the Gunners since a little child, miss the chance to see us lift the most acclaimed prize in club football? I had years on my side, and we would be back, there was no doubt about that. But to break up a partnership that had seen us fell some of Europe's elite was madness. No? As I tuned in that night, the empty space on the sofa was overwhelming, a match-day programme from Paris the only consolation of a broken European partnership...

Thomas Hills *pictured with his dad*

COLOURS
RED & WHITE

FROM MY FIRST DAY, TO MY LAST

'Jon, you're not a football fan; you're simply an Arsenal fan!' That is a phrase that has been aimed in my direction by so many people over the years! But considering my wonderful dad, Rick, as he was affectionately known to the whole family, and who sadly passed away last May, attended his first Arsenal game in 1927, even before the wonderful 1930s era, I didn't really get much choice who I supported. Red and white blood courses right through the decades and through our veins. Mind you, my dad was a little 'old school' in his thinking: One who always wanted any London side to win; an opinion that certainly hasn't been passed on down to my generation! If Arsenal can't win, do we really care who else does? As long as it isn't Tottenham, of course!

My very first memory of watching Arsenal was the semi-final against Stoke City at Hillsborough, age six. Unfortunately, another habit of my dad's was to leave five minutes before the end to beat the crowds and crush when we were children. Of course, this resulted in us missing the Peter Storey last-minute penalty equaliser to make it 2-2, as the Gunners took another step closer to clinching the first ever Double and the Cup Final win over Liverpool. I watched the final at home, as it was my sister's turn to go to the game. As a family, we had agreed a system of alternating who went with dad, but despite not going to Wembley, my memories of the day are still very vivid. As any Arsenal fan worth his salt will tell you, Charlie George scored that extra-time winner, but it is also a name that my wonderful wife Susie and I would give to our eldest son who was born in 1992—Charlie George Scutt is his name! And, of course, when our second son arrived five years later, we continued the Arsenal theme when he was baptised: Freddie Gunner Scutt, even before Mr Ljungberg had actually signed, but I hope you agree it is a classy, unique middle name and one which signals our devotion to the Arsenal.

Indeed, the priest did not actually quite absorb the importance when he baptised either son, but as it was in the same church of Our Lady of Lourdes in New Southgate where my wife and I got married in July 1991, on a totally red and white day (flowers, reception and all the wonderful bridesmaids in Arsenal-red dresses, too), he was probably just bemused, again! In fact, my wife even had 'AFC' embroidered into her wedding veil, something I'd not been aware of until she arrived at the church, which was a wonderful gesture that I'll always be thankful to Susie for.

Mind you, on our wedding day, she wasn't fully aware that one of the reasons our honeymoon was an 11-day holiday, and not the traditional 14-dayer, was to allow us to arrive back just in time for the Charity Shield clash with Spurs, and it did raise an odd eye in the following weeks when she realised. And that match is now just one of literally over a thousand I've seen since my 'debut'. But often it's the game that you can't get to when the 'Arsenal 'til I die' effect kicks in the most and the stress of not being there impacts not only you but also everyone who comes into contact with you, too.

Three generations of the Scutt family: Rick and Jon stand behind Freddie Gunner [white T-shirt] and Charlie George [black top]

My elder brother Greg once bought my wife and me a 'Highbury' sign for our home in Potters Bar, as we had mentioned how good it would be to actually 'live' at the stadium once Arsenal had moved to the new ground. And, because we made sure we sold the house to fellow Gooners, the plaque is still screwed to the front of the property, which makes me smile every time I drive past. Indeed, the sign was complemented by one of the best birthday presents I've ever received: a 3-ft tall concrete Ian Wright garden gnome, with gold tooth and all! What an ornament and what a player!

One of my most treasured Arsenal memories doesn't involve a match day, though. This one stems from the summer before we moved from Highbury, when my wife and the boys took their grandad on the tour of the stadium, nearly 80 years after he'd first visited the proud old stadium with his own father. Dad, despite his faltering health, enjoyed that day tremendously, so much so that the tour lasted about three times longer than it was supposed to. No, not because of my dad's ill health slowing him down, simply because he knew twice as much about the club than the official tour guide, who seemed delighted that my dad happily shared all his memories and knowledge with anyone who would listen as we made our way around! So, how could I be anything else but an Arsenal fan? The club has been with me since my first day and, without a doubt, will remain my companion until my very last. Arsenal 'til I die? Of course I am.

Jon Scutt

SHE LOVES YOU, YEAH YEAH YEAH!

One of my proudest Gooner moments was at The Rocket Bar a few years ago. The Rocket is a family-friendly place around the corner from Emirates where we go to meet before and after the match. Ex-England, Arsenal and Everton player Kenny Sansom had joined fans after his TV commentary had finished. I was introduced to him: 'Kenny, this is Ruby. She's a Scouser, but she's OK; she loves Arsenal, and she's one of us.' I beamed a smile from ear to ear—not for this Arsenal legend who was shaking my hand while reciting amusing moments at Goodison, but for the bona fide endorsement as a Gooner from a fellow Arsenal fanatic, who also lives, breathes and speaks Arsenal.

People ask how I grew up supporting 'the Pride of North London', 'the Kings of the South', in 1970s Liverpool, when Anfield was the capital of European football. It was like fate. My only brother was a super-talented footballer and played for Liverpool School Boys (a precursor to the youth academies at the time). I was the only sister who took an interest in his sport. At that time, the struggle for sexual equality was still to be won, so the infrastructure for modern-day women's football didn't exist.

I wasn't allowed to play (apparently it wasn't 'lady-like'), but it didn't dampen my enthusiasm for football. My brother nourished it. The sight of me sitting on a six-foot-high wall as a six-year-old watching this training session was commonplace on our Toxteth council estate. When my mum thought I was old enough, she took me to Goodison Park, for I was born into a true-blue Everton household! In one of the earliest matches I saw, Arsenal had come to town. There was excited talk of Charlie George and Arsenal's very own Georgie Best, Peter Marinello, and there was a buzz in the house because I think Everton were

rebuilding a bit of the stadium. I asked to be taken to the Arsenal end. My brother walked me from the Glawdys Street End to the away end. Gooners nodded and smiled, and I felt at home. After that, the Everton versus Arsenal fixture was my highlight of the season, like waiting for a family reunion at Christmas. The path to Goonerhood was set. I wrote to the Arsenal Supporters' Club and cherished the photocopy of squad players' autographs. My cheekier AFC friends refer to it as a calling to a land of milk and honey, 'from the scallies to the Kings', led by a lineage of foot heroes Brady, Henry and van Persie. Highbury became my place of pilgrimage.

Now it's my Evertonian family and friends who welcome me back, and, of course, Everton are my second team. The Everton versus Arsenal fixture is a special homecoming match for me with my family. But it's not always 'home, sweet home': especially if Arsenal win. I've been ridiculed and sent commemorative DVDs and T-shirts from EFC stewards to remind me that I was in their main stand as a precocious teenager named Wayne Rooney scored his wonder goal to destroy Arsenal's away record. Yet all animosity fades in our mutual hatred of Liverpool FC, who stole and wasted much of our childhood in the 70s through enforced street parties in 'Bread'-type terraced streets to celebrate yet another league or final triumph.

When I first moved to London, I was advised to ditch the Scouse accent if I wanted to get on in the company. It was quite the opposite in N5, where my pensioner friend Tony always pushed me forwards with fanfare and pride as we went through the North Bank gate. I felt like an exhibit on display. 'She's a Scouse-Gooner and grew up in Liverpool all this time on her own supporting Arsenal.' And then he'd gently prod me, 'Go on, speak, speak!' by way of infallible proof. After the wondrous response of 'Good girl!' there were always copious offers of drinks at the Gunner pub after the match.

Years later, I've got loads of great memories as a sibling of the Arsenal family. Since the early days, Arsenal have had international players, but it's true to say that Arsène Wenger has given us a global identity. I travel both home and away but enjoy it most overseas. Sometimes with others (Porto, Barcelona, Roma), sometimes alone (Milan, Turin, Alkmaar, and Paris for our Champions League final). As soon as the draw is made, I buy a language tuition DVD and learn enough to get by in the language of the host team. This not only aids communication but also creates goodwill, leaving a different impression of Arsenal fans. I also take along a small bag of AFC merchandise and traditional souvenirs of England as a gesture of thanks to hotel workers and friendly opposition fans and stewards, so they remember the game.

I speak fluent Italian, having worked there in the past. When we went to AC Milan, it was fantastic as we took over the Prima Fila restaurant in Piazza del Duomo, and the waiters were all Interisti so wanted us to win. I had a brilliant time on a four-day trip to Rome for the AS Roma match that ended in a dramatic penalty shootout. I'm very superstitious but swapped my matchday scarf with a Roma fan as a sign of goodwill at the start of the match—we went 1-0 down. I spent the rest of the match blaming myself for my change of routine. At Porto, after meticulous research, we managed to book into the hotel Arsenal had selected for their media and press conferences and two minutes away from where the squad was staying. The Camp Nou trip was a good one because with them having Messi the magician, and Fàbregas being injured, we all went for the experience rather than the final result. The fans were so friendly. There was no

animosity or arrogance, just a self-assurance that says: 'This is the way it is when the opposition comes here, what did you expect?' When I went to Paris in 2006 for our only Champions League final so far, I had a similarly positive vibe from the Barca fans.

I had bought my ticket on the Internet four days before kick-off. I spent a small fortune on that and a sport travel package for the hotel and Eurostar. It was worth every penny, but many tears were shed. I cried with pride through the opening ceremony because I just couldn't believe we were there; I cried with frustration when Lehman got sent off; I cried with joy when Sol scored; and I cried with dismay when the final whistle blew. Any Gooner will tell you that Arsenal will stir and squeeze out every emotion you have.

Closer to home for the emotional rollercoaster that was the 2005 FA Cup final at the Millennium Stadium, I stayed in the same hotel as the Arsenal squad. I remember following Gary Lewin after dinner, as he led me on a wild goose chase—he thought he'd dropped me but I doubled back on him and found him at the entrance of the AFC wing. He said the players couldn't be disturbed but would be up early the next day for a walk in the grounds. I have to admit that much of my time in between was spent in surveillance, behind my curtains, waiting for twitches of movement in the Arsenal wing; I set the alarm and was up super-early. At the crack of dawn, I saw Arsène leave for a swim and got photos upon his return. Later that day, on the way to the stadium, the players' coach arrived. I ran hard alongside it for 100 metres. Then my friends reminded me about my Achilles injury and how I wasn't supposed to run.

Running for Arsenal comes with the territory. That night in May 1989, when Michael Thomas scored his title-winning goal, I ran up the street chanting 'Champions! Champions!' My mum warned me to come in. I ignored her. The streets were deserted, as most Kopites we knew were at the match. After the second lap of the street, I went inside and closed the garden gate—just in time to hear the thud of the bricks as they rattled the woodwork behind me. On the day Arsenal were due to play Newcastle in the FA Cup final, I ran two laps (five miles) around Sefton Park in Liverpool, waving a 'Pride of London' Arsenal banner overhead. I've run 10 times around the Emirates complex for the annual 'Be a Gunner, Be a Runner' event, dressed as a nurse and pushed a hospital bed (with Arsenal bed linen) 14 miles from Emirates to Upton Park for AFC's charity of the year. I even ran four miles to Marylebone for a Gooner-Pompey informal summit to meet fans from the Portsmouth Supporters Trust before their FA Cup final against Chelsea; I'd paid for 20 lifetime memberships for fans in hardship to join the Trust, so they could get involved in saving the club they love.

Sharing a joke or two, being entertained and composing both our club's history and future is what it's all about for fans. Gooners are truly fanatics for Arsenal, so much so that every couple of seasons I undertake professional modelling photo shoots of me in AFC gear; I even have had personalised Royal Mail stamps showing me proudly wearing my Arsenal shirts or hugging van Persie! I use these to post mail to friends all over the world, and people love them. And when I went to Downing Street last month, I wore my Arsenal jacket and badge, taking Arsenal to the corridors of power.

I have images and memories engrained in my mind that distil the essence of Goonerhood. These include: watching Henry score the first goal against Southampton on the giant pitch screen at Highbury; Pires' 'it's delightful, it's delectable' chip in the rain in front of me at Anfield; van Persie being introduced to Gooners wearing weird tight, stripy pants at the final match against Leicester in our invincible 2003/04 unbeaten season; Teddy Sheringham's knowing glance as he caught me enviously observing West Ham fans at the Clock End when they became the last team to beat us at Highbury; and every single Middlesbrough player with his head dropped after Arsenal came back to win 5-3 at the start of the 2004/05 season.

At the Ladies' final of the French Open tennis tournament in July 2009, a Gooner had been sold a seat right in front of mine. He looked at my Arsenal shirt, and we shook hands warmly. Perhaps that gesture conveys best what it is to be Gooner—a psychic bond that unifies us and a helping hand from fate.

Ruby Dixon

THE GREAT ESCAPE

Where were you when Michael Thomas scored that goal? I was there! I'd taken the day off work and hired a white XR2 for the day, which was really extravagant, but I got a good deal from the lads who leased our vans. Me and Lanky Dave (I'm 6'3"; Lanky Dave was even taller, so his nickname wasn't ironic) left with what we thought was plenty of time to get there. We didn't have tickets, but we just thought we'd have to get there and see what happened then. I don't really know why Dave wanted to come; he was a Derby County supporter, but he liked a pint and was always good company. We got caught up in the traffic on the motorway. I used to be a van driver back then, doing deliveries all over the country, so I thought I'd be clever and take a detour. I didn't have a map; it was all instinct. We got very, very lost but finally arrived at an eerily quiet Anfield, which confused us. We had no idea the kick-off had been delayed. That's when a young lad asked if we were looking for tickets, and after some downwards negotiating, we paid £20 each, although after handing over the money my heart sank when I saw they were for the Kop end! Oh well, in for a penny, eh!

We stood about halfway up the Kop, 10 metres from the exit, just in case, and tried really hard not to speak. Lanky Dave was OK, he was northern sounding, but I knew I sounded Cockney to the locals, even though I'm from Borehamwood. So I said nothing, just nodded and smiled when I needed to. But then Smudger scored! I jumped slightly, but styled it nicely into a 180-degree turn. Fortunately for me, the home fans' attention was drawn to a small group of younger lads who were sitting up on the dividing barrier and had cheered as the goal went in. There were some vocal threats and lots of muttering, but nothing materialised. However, I realised I would have to behave.

In truth, and despite the goal, I doubted we would score the second goal and win the title. I assumed Liverpool would get an equaliser, if I'm honest, but, if we could hang on, it would still show that we could

beat them at their place and weren't just there to make up the numbers. But as the game went on, Liverpool seemed more nervous; Arsenal were in the driving seat. We still couldn't do it, though. I had convinced myself of that so that I wouldn't be too disappointed. The last moments of the game are a blur. I remember jumping into the air but can't recall my feet hitting the floor, until about three steps from the top in the exit staircase. As I'd launched into a celebratory 'YEEEESSS!', Lanky Dave had grabbed me and shoved me along the row and off towards the escape route. I don't think I've ever run so fast. We found the car eventually after frantically looking down a few wrong streets. We jumped in, locked the doors behind us and sped off. It was at a set of lights on the main road out of the city that it started to sink in. A van pulled up alongside us, the horn was tooting madly. I looked around to see a load of Gooners inside; their party had started and the van was rocking. I didn't realise that Dave was waving my scarf at every vehicle we'd passed, but it was brilliant. We stopped off for a pint somewhere off the motorway, not far out of Liverpool, somewhere I thought was far enough away to be safe. But as I was locking the car, I saw Lanky Dave entering the pub with my Arsenal scarf tied around his forehead. I tried to call him back, but he didn't hear. As I ran through the door, expecting carnage, I was struck by how quiet the pub was. Everyone was staring at Dave. 'Two pints of Best, please, landlord,' said Dave. As he started to pour, the barman asked, 'Been to the match then, lads?' I said that we had, still fearful it was about to kick off. 'Nice one,' said the landlord. 'This is a Blue pub... these are on me!' Friday 26 May 1989. At Anfield. It was a fantastic night. An unforgettable night. It was the best night of my life.

Mark Herron

GREEN LINE TO REDS

I have enjoyed many highs and not a few lows in my time as a supporter of Arsenal (call me an old fogey, but I've never taken to the term 'Gooner'), not least being the joy of leaving White Hart Lane after a great strike from Ray Kennedy secured a 1-0 win and the title, the first part of the Double, at the end of the 1970/71 season. The following Saturday at Wembley, the nail-biting extra-time and the tumultuous feeling of euphoria leaving the match were wonderful indeed. I had thought I would never repeat the elation of the previous year, riding the Tube home after the scintillating 3-0 win over Anderlecht to secure the Inter Cities Fairs Cup, but the Double week topped that by a mile.

Only 12 months later, the lowest point, Alan Clarke's goal denying us a consecutive FA Cup and the depressing trip home. Subsequent successes have never quite provided the same sensational feeling, nor failures quite the same sinking sensation, but maybe those extremes of emotion are the preserve of the younger supporter. Certainly, the club has enjoyed much success and now plays a brand of football admired everywhere, yet those moments remain the pinnacle of emotional memory.

But it is the start of the journey that I remember in some ways more clearly, in other ways far more vaguely, than any of the years since. I was eight years old and had been excited all week because I was to be taken to my first football match. Dressed presumably sensibly, my mother and I walked down the road to the bus stop and got on a 351 bus to the centre of Watford, where we got on a private hire bus. I remember particularly that it was a Green Line Coach, a single-decker with an unusual smell inside. It was the first time I had been on a Green Line as they were normally long-distance express services that went to places like East Grinstead and were far too expensive to ride on for the bus trips I usually made as a child.

We set off and, in what seemed like no time at all, arrived alongside what to me was an incredibly high brick wall where the coach parked. I learned later that this was Drayton Park. It seemed an immensely wide road and full of people decked out in red and white. As we made our way from the coach to the end of the road and turned right, I saw huge crowds coming from the Underground and disappearing into an entrance just ahead. Passing lots of sellers of rattles and scarves and other souvenirs, we in turn entered the lane towards the North Bank, and, among lots of tall people, we got through the turnstiles. My mother then decided it was too crowded to go on the terrace with me, so we went through another turnstile to transfer to the unreserved seating area in the East Stand.

I remember the excitement building and building, and then the teams came out to roars of support the like of which I had never heard before. I remember very little of what followed, though so much of the game has been written of since that all those details can be looked up, and I could not truly say that it was my memory and not what I have read since that I would be recounting. What I did remember most, though, was the acceptance of defeat with good nature all around me, praise for the opposition and their quality of play and hope for the future with the fight shown by the Arsenal side. I knew then that Arsenal would be the only club I could possibly support, and so it has been.

Why does so much stick in my mind from 52 years ago? Because only five days later, that day's opponents went to Belgrade and many never made the return trip beyond Munich. Arsenal lost that match 4-5, the last match played in England by Matt Busby's Babes. Following Munich and United's gallant effort to fulfil their commitments for the rest of that season, many friends of mine became United supporters, never going to Old Trafford but claiming they supported the best team in the land. I stayed with Arsenal, went to Highbury regularly and saw, week in, week out, the players I supported—and that's how I'll remain, forever.

Mike Burgess

IT'S A KNOCKOUT

Arsenal were playing Liverpool in the last game of the season and needed to win 2-0 to take the title. It was the game of ALL games. But my ex-wife had arranged for a visit to her parents, who lived about 150 miles away, and I was forced to drop her off there, just 90 minutes before the kick-off. Not only had I not got a ticket, but this detour complicated things even further for me. Urging her into the car, I drove like a maniac, but despite the speeding offences, we still arrived about 15 minutes after kick-off. Neglecting the hugs and hellos, I rushed straight towards the TV and settled down to agonise like every other Gooner on the planet. Halftime came, and I got myself a large, stiff drink and prepared for the next half. Arsenal scored, and a sense of fate passed through me. Time went on, and I found myself living on whatever nerves I had left. I didn't know about the lads on the pitch, but I was nearing exhaustion. It was clear my behaviour was not acceptable to the in-laws, who decided to ignore me, which suited me just fine as the game wore on. Suddenly Michael Thomas was clear. 'It's up for grabs...' I leapt into the air and... Well, you see, the in-laws lived in a posh, listed, thatched cottage, full of low beams which were a major feature in the spacious and luxurious lounge area, and when I had leapt up to celebrate Arsenal's second goal, my head smashed into one of the centuries-old lumps of timber. When I eventually came round, my head was pounding, and I could barely recognise the people standing over me, but my first words were: 'Did we win?' Feeling the bloodied lump on my head, I saw the ex smiling, and she told me that she didn't know as I'd been out cold for over 15 minutes, and they'd turned the TV off when they'd realised my injury. Rushing to the TV, I switched it back on, only to find the broadcast had finished, so, believe it or not, I couldn't find out the result until the next morning. As soon as I found out the brilliant news, my injury paled into insignificance, along with the concussion. Come on you Reds!

Dave Wyatt

BRAVE OR FOOLISH?

Back in 1968, age 11, I found myself at a rugby-playing grammar school, and, although the majority of the boys were football fanatics, we were forced to take up egg-chasing and made to enjoy the experience. It emerged that I was fairly good at the sport and was fortunate enough to make the first team on a regular basis, and games were usually played on a Saturday morning.

The problem was that I was a Highbury-born-and-bred Arsenal fanatic, whose family included many uncles with season tickets, and we never missed a home game together. And when the FA Cup came around each season, one of my uncles would always treat my brother and me to away trips. So, when the 1968/69 fifth round draw was made, and the Gunners were paired with West Bromwich Albion at The Hawthorns, I immediately knew that we'd be making the trip to the Black Country. Unfortunately, though, there was the matter of a school rugby fixture to navigate, and I had the awkward task of informing the games teacher that I would be unavailable for selection that particular Saturday. He didn't take the news too well at all. Horrified, he sent me straight to the headmaster's office, where I was reminded all about 'school loyalty' and the fact that, in his opinion at least, school duties came before the Arsenal. Not to me they didn't, and I told him so. But, despite my pleas, I was given an ultimatum: 'If you go to watch Arsenal, you'll never play first-team rugby for the school again!' To me there was no real choice: WEST BROM, HERE WE COME! I informed the headmaster and the games teacher of my decision. However, there was a twist.

It is a little-known fact that Saturday 12 February 1969 was the first date in FA Cup history where the entire fifth round fixture list was lost to the weather—heavy snow across the whole country saw almost every sporting fixture fall to the harsh conditions, including the rugby match I was originally supposed to be playing in. I didn't know whether to laugh or cry!

So, even though I didn't travel to West Brom after all, and the rugby match was postponed, I was still banished, never to play for the First XI again—a punishment that saw me miss several important rugby tours and cup successes along the way. Looking back, 40 years on, I think I was either very brave or very foolish, but at the time, it was the most natural thing in the world to do. However, I often wonder whether, with the gift of hindsight, I would make the same decision again. My answer is always the same, though... COME ON YOU GUNNERS!

Paul Milesi *pictured with his sons at Wembley*

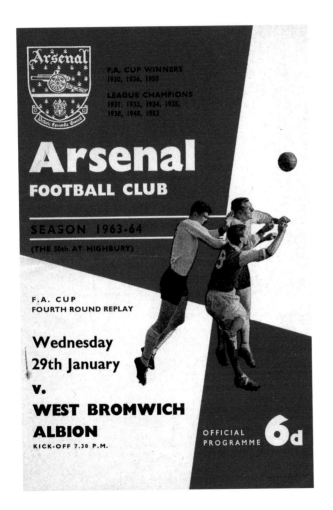

F.A. CUP WINNERS
1930, 1936, 1950

LEAGUE CHAMPIONS
1931, 1933, 1934, 1935, 1938, 1948, 1953

Arsenal
FOOTBALL CLUB

SEASON 1963-64

(THE 50th AT HIGHBURY)

F.A. CUP
FOURTH ROUND REPLAY

Wednesday 29th January

v.

WEST BROMWICH ALBION

KICK-OFF 7.30 P.M.

OFFICIAL PROGRAMME **6d**

MY FIRST AWAY DAY

My father took me to my first game at the age of seven, and I can remember it so well: a 3-1 defeat to Luton Town in March 1957. Our goal was scored by Derek Tapscott, who drilled it in from the edge of the area, but I cried all the way home because we lost. However, the setback did not put me off, and my dad took me regularly to all the home and local away games, but then, in 1963, Arsenal were drawn away to West Bromwich Albion in the FA Cup, and I just had to go and so told my parents the news! How things have changed over the years, as my mother actually went and bought me a train ticket and was happy to see her 14-year-old son go off to Birmingham, totally on his own. Can you imagine that happening nowadays?

I arrived at St Pancras station and was amazed that I was not alone. There were thousands of Gooners (although in those days the name didn't exist!), and any nerves I had were soon gone. I settled into a seat with magazines and papers and couldn't wait for the match, but then it dawned on me. I had no idea where to get off or, more importantly, where in Birmingham West Brom actually was! After what seemed an eternity, we stopped at a station where most, but not all, Arsenal fans got off. So I did the same and found myself walking behind a group of fans all the way to the ground. As it was not an all-ticket match, you could stand anywhere you wanted, but I was worried about where I should go. But then, once inside, from the corner flag to the halfway line it was packed with Arsenal fans. And I thought I would be one of only a few there!

Although it was not a great era for Arsenal, our team tore into West Brom, and we were 3-1 up at the break. I was really enjoying myself. In the second half, my hero of the time, Vic Groves, got concussed, but in those days there were no subs, so he just played on. West Brom then got a second, then a third, and with their crowd going mad, Arsenal were really hanging on. I remember for the first time supporting Arsenal being totally scared that the other team were going to score the winner. Somehow we hung on for a replay at Highbury, and, as we left the ground, I was so relieved. An announcement came over that the station for Arsenal fans had changed. I had no idea where that was and now was really worried. I asked a group of lads a few years older than me if they knew where to go, and they took me under their wing and got me to the station just in time for the last train back. We had a carriage to ourselves, and the trip back was wonderful. My new-found friends were so funny that I laughed all the way back to London. My parents, who met me at the station, seemed very relieved to see me, and I couldn't wait to tell them about my big adventure, which was the start of me going to all the away games with my new gang of friends. Nowadays, though, it's home games only for me, although my father, who has been going since 1927 and is now 90, still comes with me.

Nigel Tremlett

WATCHING HISTORY

"TURF" CIGARETTES

REG. LEWIS
ARSENAL

50   FOOTBALLERS   Nº25

I do not remember much about the first time I saw Arsenal, because I was only eight at the time, but the match was at White Hart Lane in 1943, and I went with my 10-year-old friend, Barry Levy. After that, we went regularly to watch both teams that played on that ground! We both enjoyed the atmosphere and the adventure of the bombings that were going on in London at that time. Then, at the end of the war, at the grand old age of 10, I realised I would have to make a decision that could have a great bearing on the rest of my life. I lived in Cranwich Road, near Stamford Hill, and calculated that Highbury was the nearest ground to me, and I also convinced my father that he should give up his allegiance to West Ham, which dated back to the famous White Horse Final at Wembley in 1923. In becoming Arsenal fans, we became real black sheep as most members of our family supported Tottenham. In fact, that rivalry with my cousins still remains, although they have been rather quiet until very, very recently.

My earliest vivid memory of watching Arsenal was in 1945 when we played Dynamo Moscow. I was so excited at the prospect of seeing the great Stanley Matthews playing for Arsenal, together with Stan Mortensen and many other guest players. It was a midweek game, and I told my headmaster that I would not be in school because I had a hospital appointment with my mother.

When Barry and I got to the ground, we were horrified to find that a thick smog had descended on the area and visibility was down to about 50 feet. Although the game was played to the final whistle, Arsenal lost 4-3, and we hardly saw any of the play. There were accusations at the time that the Russians had 12 players on the field because the referee could only see about a quarter of the pitch, but if defeat wasn't bad enough, worse was to follow when the newspapers printed photos of disappointed supporters leaving the ground, and I featured in one of them. The following day, my headmaster asked how my mother was, before showing me the picture. I think I still have the marks where he demonstrated his disapproval!

By the time I went to Wembley to see Arsenal beat Liverpool in the 1950 Cup final, I was already a season ticket holder. My late father purchased four tickets at the beginning of the 1948/49 season for us, my uncle and cousin. The final was a fantastic occasion, and we won by two great goals scored by Reg Lewis, which I am always reminded of when I approach the Emirates and see his profile on the stadium. Believe it or not, there were only three 'foreign' players in that team: Alex Forbes and Jimmy Logie of Scotland and Walley Barnes of Wales, Arsenal legends one and all. Talking of Arsenal legends, I also clearly remember my cricketing hero, Denis Compton, playing on the left wing and taking a corner which enabled his brother, Leslie, to score the equalising goal against Chelsea in the semi-final at White Hart Lane. It was in the dying minutes, and Leslie kept coming forward against the wishes of the captain, Joe Mercer, who kept gesturing for him to stay back. Incidentally, I believe that Leslie was the oldest player to receive his first England cap, at the ripe old age of 38. I have to say that the memory of my first visit to the old Wembley will always live with me, not just because of the atmosphere that was generated by both sets of supporters, but also the friendliness between both inside and outside the ground. There was something extra special about seeing the twin towers and feeling part of the history that was being made.

Irving Graham

MY GREAT GRANDAD

I am a 17-year-old Arsenal fan and have been following the Gunners since the age of five, when I attended my first Arsenal game, and my time following the 'best football club in the world' has brought with it an exceptional number of memories and stories that have undoubtedly affected my life and who I am today. In the early years, it was just my grandad and me. He's been a fan for over 60 years and has come through thick and thin. Grandad had always wanted a son, so when I came along and began to show an interest in football, he did his best to get me hooked. I am told I have given him a new lease of life and new-found love, which is difficult for me to describe, as I am so proud of the fact. Grandad has been to every single Arsenal game with me and has demonstrated outstanding commitment on many occasions, genuinely enjoying not only watching the matches, but also taking his grandson along and sharing the experience. Grandad is truly an inspirational figure.

During the middle years, I struggled to attend as many games due to living abroad, but I was still able to attend a couple of games and was well-informed of Arsenal's successes as we went a season unbeaten. My grandad still attended the games and, as has been the tradition for the past eight years, bought and kept a copy the programmes for my return. I feel spoilt to have such a wonderful grandad.

In recent years, the experiences of Arsenal matches have considerably altered. I not only go with my grandad now, but also with two of my best friends who are as whole-hearted Arsenal as me. Furthermore, I feel the roles between my grandad and me are slowly reversing as I can now, gladly, return the favour of looking after him when we go to the matches. I realise how privileged I am to watch The Arsenal week in, week-out, with my grandad.

Jack Elkins *pictured with his grandad*

19

MY MUSEUM PIECE

My grandfather, Charles Stairs, was born in 1863 in Manchester, although the family subsequently moved to South London where he eventually became involved in the munitions trade and attended his first Arsenal match in 1886. My dad, William, also became a staunch supporter in due course and regularly attended Highbury when football began again after the Great War, so, by the time I was born and was old enough to begin my own interesting football, he was able to regale great stories about Arsenal's wonderful teams from yesteryear, which included legendary players such as Cliff Basten, Ted Drake, Alex James and Herbert Chapman. The dice was cast and for me, then and now, it's Arsenal forever! Dad started taking me to matches in the 1950s. Travelling in from leafy Dorking was so exciting for a young lad, and the train journeys up to Waterloo, the Underground ride to Arsenal and the walk up towards the exit with thousands of other fans is still a vivid and treasured memory.

The sights and sounds as we approached the stadium made the excitement levels tangible—policemen on horseback, ticket touts, hot dog stands with their delicious-smelling fried onions, and stalls selling scarves, badges and rattles lined the route to the turnstiles, where fans formed orderly queues. Once inside and packed in like sardines on the sweeping terraces, I waited anxiously until the first big roar from the crowd signalled the arrival of the teams from the tunnel. Dad and I continued our lovely Arsenal ritual until 1964, when I joined the Royal Navy, meaning I was abroad for long periods. Indeed, I was in Hong Kong when dad died in 1975, but I knew we had been together and shared some wonderful moments, including celebrating the Double in 1971—boy did we celebrate!

Some years after my father died, I unearthed a copy of the Sunday Graphic newspaper from September 1935, which ran a report from Arsenal's opening game to the season against Sunderland. The paper also featured a crowd photo, and you can imagine my delight when I spotted dad's face, carrying a lovely smile,

right in the middle of the shot! I treasure this photo and took it along to the Arsenal museum on the 75th anniversary of my father's photo, where I handed it over to the lovely staff that seemed amazed and delighted that my family have been watching the club for over 125 years. Arsenal has brought the Stairs family so many happy memories over the years and hopefully will continue to do so long into the future.

Peter Stairs

ASHBURTON DAYS

We lived at 55 Ashburton Grove, a dead-end street that had the council tip, a coal and scrap metal yards at the bottom of it. My uncle Bill had the house before us, but he was killed in Italy during World War II. The street was our football pitch, and all the lads would be out playing. Our only interruption was when the dustcarts rumbled past on their way to the tip!

My nan and grandad's house was on the corner and was like a café; they used to cook for the family, which included uncle Joe, who lived with us. There would be three sittings most days, all made on an old range. Nan was a fantastic cook. In the mornings, it was my job to clean out all the ash from the cooker and put it on the runner beans in the back garden. My grandad used to give me some of his ration cards, then send me off to the shop to buy sweets with them. He would always warn me, though: 'Don't you dare eat any on the way back, I know exactly how many I get in a quarter!'

On Saturday mornings, grandad gave me a folded piece of paper with money inside, and I used to take it to man at the bottom of Queensland Road on the Y-junction under the lamp post. He was the bookie's runner—gambling was illegal back then. I also ran errands for nan, running up to Jackson's paper shop, or to Davises grocers and dairy. In return, nan would sometimes treat me to the football.

Mum and stepdad got married, and we moved to Benwell Road. I got on very well with my stepdad, and he took me to Highbury regularly from 1953. There were 15 of us from several families who used to stand together at the Clock End. And, because I was still so small, one of my uncles, who was a carpenter, made me a box to stand on so that I could stand alongside the rest of the family by 'our' crash barrier. Sadly, there are now only 3 of that 15 who are still alive.

I continued having to earn my football entrance money by doing odd jobs, including things like collecting empty lemonade and beer bottles and taking them back to The Favourite pub at the top of Queensland Road, which used to earn us a penny a bottle, or, when they dug the cobbles up to put tarmac down our road, he sold the tar blocks to local people to use on their fires. No central heating in those days!

Ashburton Grove was a place where everyone knew and helped one another. All the houses where kids lived would have a key on a piece of string so that they could let themselves in after school; nobody ever got robbed. Another thing I remember about the street was the man who used to come along on his bike every evening and light the gas-lamps with a flame on the end of a long pole. Our school was at the top of the street, which had a playground on the roof, surrounded by a very high fence, but not quite high enough to stop our football from flying over on regular occasions!

I met and married a local girl, from Rock Street, Finsbury Park, and we have two Arsenal-loving sons, Mark and Jason, and, after a long and distinguished career in the Army where I rose to Sergeant Major, I am now delighted to work at the Arsenal museum, where I sometimes feel more like an exhibit than an employee! For an Arsenal fanatic like myself, the job is a dream come true, as from my position on the front desk, I look out over our amazing new stadium, which sits on the site which holds so many fond memories of growing up and my youth—and where the players run out on the pitch, well, that used to be my bedroom!

Bill Savage *pictured with his family in the garden of 55 Ashburton Grove*

ARSENAL 'TIL I DIED:
BILL WHITEHEAD (1886-1964)

I guess my reason for supporting the Arsenal is a bit different to most fans'. It all started three weeks after I was born. My dad, George, worked as an engine driver in the Royal Arsenal, specifically in the Dial Square workshop. When David Danskin asked around if anyone fancied forming a football team dad said 'yes' and had the honour of playing in the club's first ever game. He would tell me and my brother Syd this story for years. We were a bit sceptical as there were loads of other blokes in the area that made the same claim. They got away with it as no one knew of any records that said they did or didn't. Either way, dad was a big fan of Royal Arsenal and used to go to as many games as he could. Even in his later days he would talk about the great players of the past such as Peter Connolly, Bill Julian and Fred Beardsley.

Dad took me to my first game in 1893. Not only was it my first game, it was the first game under the new name of Woolwich Arsenal and the club's first ever League game. There was a big crowd at the Manor Ground that day, and they went bonkers when the Reds went 2-0 up. Even though the game finished 2-2 we went home happy having witnessed our first league point. Dad would take me occasionally but it became difficult when the Boer War started as he had to work overtime on Saturday afternoons. Once the war was over, he took me and Syd to every home game and we stood on the Kop at the Abbey Road end of the ground.

When I was about 15, dad took me and Syd to buy a bike. The owner of the bike shop was none other than David Danskin! Dad introduced us to Mr Danskin who told us that we should be proud of our dad who had indeed played in that very first game. He showed us a scrapbook including a newspaper cutting with dad's name in it! Syd and I lived on that story for years and would often get a drink bought for us in the

Lord Derby. My best moment as an Arsenal fan was in 1904 when we won promotion to the First Division. Harry Bradshaw had built a fantastic team that would often completely overrun the opposition. Tommy Shanks and Tim Coleman were ruthless up front, and Jimmy Ashcroft was the best goalkeeper I ever saw at the club.

Because Plumstead was a bit of an outpost, we used to see the players regularly in the town. It was great because it was like they were our mates. Some of them took the fans' hospitality a little too far though. Peter Kyle was sold because he overindulged once too often and spent a night in the cells.

Dad had hoped that Syd and I would follow him into working at the Royal Arsenal but during the early 1900s, they had mass redundancies. I got a job working in a factory making parts for telephones, which were starting to become popular. Money was good, so I got down to the Manor Ground for most home games and went to the occasional away game, including a couple of those organised by the infamous Torpedo Boys before they were moved up to Glasgow.

When Henry Norris moved us to Highbury, I carried on going although Syd couldn't make every game because his wages as a cleaner weren't that great. It was a fair old journey, and, when there was a big crowd, going to a game would take all day as the queues for trams in Blackstock Road seemed to go on forever.

After nearly 40 years of following Arsenal, I finally got to see them win something. I was one of the lucky ones who got a ticket for the FA Cup final in 1930. By this time, I'd moved to Harrow, so getting to Highbury was a bit easier. Even better was that I got to see the great team of the 1930s. Alex James was a master of the game, and watching him and Cliff Bastin work together was a joy to behold.

After the war, I struggled to get to games but still followed the team in the newspapers. It was a shame seeing them go into decline in the late 1950s, and by the time I died in 1964 things were really bad. Hopefully, they'll pick up again in a few years' time, and my grandchildren can enjoy the good times that I witnessed. Arsenal 'til I died.

Andy Kelly

Contributors

This book was developed, designed and produced by David Lane at Legends Publishing. Other contributors include:

Charlie George
Adam Velasco
Laurence Kingsley
Peter Clydesdale
Stephen Rusbridge
Big Raddy
Terry Robinson
James Purcell
Gary the Gooner
Brad Duncan
Peter Rapley
Sarah Rooney
Bernard Chaplin
Arsenal Whittick
Yongbeom Kim
Tony Attwood
Shaun Fuller
Steve Cowan
Paul Reynolds
Atiyah Meadows
Tim Sylvester
Joe Hurd

Mary O'Shea
Debbie Freeland
Thomas Hills
Jon Scutt
Ruby Dixon
Renato Santana
De Olivera
Agit
Tony Allan
Mark Herron
Mike Burgess

Dave Wyatt
Paul Milesi
Nigel Tremlett
Irving Graham
Jack Elkins
Peter Stairs
Bill Savage
Irfan Master
Kate Laurens
Andy Kelly
Samir Singh

If, after reading this book, you feel you have an Arsenal story to tell and would like to contribute to 'Arsenal 'Til I Die 2', please e-mail david@legendspublishing.net.

WWW.TILIDIE.CO.UK

Credits

Copy Editing: Elizabeth Evans
Layout: David Lane
Typesetting: Eva Feldmann
Cover Design: David Lane